Making
Sense of History

Peter Skagestad

Making Sense of History

*The Philosophies of Popper
and Collingwood*

Universitetsforlaget

Oslo — Bergen — Tromsø

© The Norwegian Research Council for Science and the Humanities 1975
Section A.79.24-15T
ISBN 82-00-01460-6
Cover design by Terje Myhrvold

Printed in Norway by
Joh. Nordahls Trykkeri, Oslo

Preface

In the course of writing my Ph.D. dissertation on R. G. Collingwood's theory of presuppositions, I briefly explored in an Epilogue the parallels and contrasts between Collingwood's analysis of presuppositions and Karl Popper's analysis of historical knowledge. This theme was further developed in a course of lectures given at Brandeis University in the spring term of 1973 and privately circulated since May 1973 as a typescript entitled 'Critical philosophy of history'. The present essay is based largely on these lectures, though the discussion has been considerably expanded.

Inevitably, there is some overlap with my dissertation (now privately published as *Collingwood's Theory of Presuppositions*, Oslo, 1974), especially in the sections dealing specifically with Collingwood. Equally inevitably, I have in the meantime changed my mind on certain points; my present attitude is on the whole more critical of Collingwood than it was in the earlier work. However, this essay is not intended as a sequel to my dissertation; my primary objective has been to give a self-contained presentation of certain issues.

The thoughts presented here originally grew out of numerous discussions with Professor Alasdair MacIntyre, to whom I shall always be indebted. The manuscript of this essay has been read by Dr. Guttorm Fløistad and Dr. Alastair Hannay, both of whom have contributed valuable comments and criticisms. For all remaining imperfections I am solely responsible.

In writing this essay, I was motivated by an interest in historical method, both for its own sake and insofar as it provides a 'touchstone' for certain important and influential views in epistemology. It is hoped that my discussion of these views may be of some interest to philosophers and historians alike.

Oslo, January 1975
Peter Skagestad

5

Contents

Introduction

It has been the tradition to subdivide philosophy into disciplines according to the type of questions asked, the methods applied in answering them, and the criteria on which the answer is judged satisfactory or not. Such time-honored disciplines are logic, ethics, metaphysics, ontology, and epistemology. These are not presumed to differ in respect of subject-matter; commonly, one and the same problem may be discussed from the vantage point of any one of these disciplines. Consider a typical piece of discourse drawn from the literature of ethics: 'God has created us; hence, we ought to obey His will.' With regard to this proposition a number of questions may be raised. Does the conclusion 'We ought to obey God's will' validly follow from the premise 'God has created us'? In general, can normative statements ever follow from statements of fact? These are questions of logic. Does God exist? More generally, can existence be ascribed to that realm of immaterial being to which God is thought to belong? These are questions of metaphysics, or of ontology. What kind of evidence can we have for the claim that God has created us? What kind of evidence can we have for claims concerning God's will? Are these the kind of things we can claim to know at all? These are questions of epistemology. The questions of the nature of our obligation toward our creator and of the nature of obligations in general are questions of ethics; but this is not because these questions concern something which may be termed 'the subject-matter of ethics'; the same subject-matter may give rise to questions within any one of the traditional philosophical disciplines.

In recent decades, however, a new classification of philosophical disciplines has emerged, by which the disciplines are distinguished according to their subject-matter, and not according to types of question or criteria for solutions. Examples are the philosophy of language, the philosophy of science, the philosophy of history, and the philosophy of religion. It is important to note that, because the old classification cuts across subject-matter, this new classification cuts across the old one. The failure to appreciate this fact creates problems in applying the new classification, and in characterizing each discipline in a rational and fruitful manner.

These problems appear most clearly in the internal-external dispute in the philosophy of science. One approach in the philosophy of science consists in taking the rationality of science for granted, and restricting the philosophical inquiry to examining the logic of scientific explanation. Proponents of this *internalist* approach are Nagel, Hempel, Feigl, and, more ambiguously, Popper. A different approach lies in questioning the rationality of the entire scientific enterprise, on ethical or epistemological grounds. Proponents of this *externalist* approach are Kuhn, Feyerabend, and Habermas. Now the situation is, that for the strict internalist, the problems occupying the externalist are not real problems at all; the externalist does not seem to him to be doing philosophy of science, as he understands it, and he feels no need to take seriously the criticisms advanced by the externalist. Conversely, the externalist – notably Habermas – feels no need to meet the internalist on his own ground, or to take seriously the questions concerning the logic of scientific explanation, since these questions seem to arise only on the assumption of the essential rationality of science. Yet there are no doubt substantive disagreements between, say, Feigl and Habermas: for instance, the former believes that science progresses rationally, the latter does not. But the issue is prevented from coming out into the forum of discussion. In this way the different conceptions of what the philosophy of science is conceal substantive issues within the philosophy of science. There is no need for an elaborate theory of 'the incommensurability of conceptual schemes' to account for this situation; what is needed is the simple recognition that the problems in the philosophy of science cut across the traditional classification of philosophical disciplines. The specific focus of one's approach is largely a matter of one's interests and one's qualifications: an interest in, and an aptitude for, studies in the logic of explanation need not preclude a questioning attitude toward the rationality of the canons observed by scientists; nor, conversely, need the latter attitude preclude an interest in the question of how the rules of logic apply to scientific explanation, on the supposition that certain canons are accepted.

Similar problems arise in the philosophy of history; here the boundary line is commonly drawn between 'speculative' and 'analytical' philosophy of history. Initially, this distinction may be explained by the ambiguity of the word 'history', which may be taken either in the sense of the course of human events (*res gestae*), or in the sense of the intellectual activity of studying the course of human events (*historia rerum gestarum*). Speculative philosophy of history conceives its subject-matter as history in the first sense; its practitioners typically ask questions about whether the course of history, in this sense, marks a progress in human affairs, and whether its motive forces are mental or material. These questions are partly metaphysical and partly, it seems, empirical, thus bordering on the domain of history proper; not uncommonly, therefore, speculative philosophers of history have been accused of a priori armchair history. Analytical philosophy of history, on the other hand, conceives of history in the second sense as its subject-matter; its proponents typically ask logical questions concerning the form of historical explanation, epistemological questions concerning the reliability of historical evidence, and semantic questions concerning the interpretation of terms occurring in historical narratives. Examples of these two approaches are, on the one hand, Taine's claim that human events are caused by physical conditions, and on the other hand, Hempel's insistence that historical explanations are implicitly deductive, in that they make tacit reference to general laws.

This simple division of the philosophy of history into speculative and analytical is, for various reasons, unsatisfactory. Even if history as an intellectual activity is chosen as one's subject-matter (a choice which, as I intend to show, is in itself problematic), this choice does not dictate one and only one approach to the subject. As was noted, the traditional philosophical disciplines cut across divisions of subject-matter; thus, given a particular subject-matter, a variety of approaches remain open. I wish, in particular, to distinguish two 'nonspeculative' approaches to the philosophy of history; let us call them 'analytical' and 'critical'. Analytical philosophers of history, whether deductivists like Hempel, or nondeductivists like Donagan and Dray, are essentially agnostic as regards the judgments of historians. The assumption is that the historians are doing their job the way it should be done; the task of the philosopher is merely the logical or semantic elucidation of the explanations actually produced by historians. It is true that, after Hempel published his original paper in 1942, he was accused of the hubris of telling historians how to run their business. The important fact to note, however, is that Hempel readily accepted the criticism as relevant, and proceeded to try and prove it wrong by trying to show that his deductive model provided a useful 'explication' or 'rational reconstruction' of actual historical explanations.[1]

It will be instructive to consider the analytical analogues to the questions raised by speculative philosophers, of whether history progresses, and whether its motive forces are mental or material. According to Hempel, the historian explains an event causally by relating it to a set of necessary and sufficient conditions, subsumed under a general law. Instead of asking 'Are the motive forces of history mental or material?', what the philosopher must ask is, 'What kind of necessary and sufficient conditions do historians specify in their explanations? Do they specify such things as motives and beliefs, or such things as physical or economic circumstances?' Obviously, the answer will not be 'The motive forces are mental' or 'The motive forces are material', but 'According to the historians, the motive forces, etc.' Criticizing Hempel, Dray has insisted that historical explanations are not causal, but rational; they are 'how possibly' and not 'why necessarily' explanations.[2] That is to say, one explains an event by relating it to certain canons of rationality, in the light of which it becomes intelligible. Now one may ask, 'How do historians render an event intelligible? Do they relate it to our own present canons of rationality, to those peculiar to the age in question, or to certain timeless canons?' In the first case, historians will necessarily present history as progress, in the second, they will necessarily deny the possibility of progress, and in the third, they may or may not assert that progress, as a matter of empirical fact, has taken place. In each case, the philosopher's answer to the question of progress must inevitably be prefixed by 'According to the historians'.

In the approach which I have called 'critical', the logical and semantic analysis of historical explanations is merely ancillary to the main task of raising, first, the epistemological question of whether historical explanations constitute real knowledge, second, the metaphysical question of what constitutes the world of historical experience (i.e. whether it is physical events, thoughts, feelings, or whatnot).

In other words, the critical philosopher of history is not only interested in knowing how historians explain events, he is also interested in knowing whether their procedures are justified, which amounts to examining both the nature of knowledge and the nature of the world which we claim to have knowledge about. Faced with a nondeductive historical explanation, a critical philosopher will not be content merely to ascertain that it is nondeductive; he will go on to ask, 'Are nondeductive inferences valid?' Faced with a 'how possibly' explanation which invokes timeless canons of rationality, he will ask whether there are, in fact, timeless canons of rationality. To the extent that he answers these questions in the negative, he will have to reject the historical explanation here offered to him. His attitude toward historians, in short, is not agnostic, but critical.

One obvious question is: can one criticize historians without being oneself an historian? In my opinion, one cannot, provided 'historian' is taken to mean 'someone knowledgeable about history', not 'member of a History Department.' But I do not wish at this stage to prejudge the question of *how* one criticizes historical explanations; essential to the enterprise of critical philosophy is only the conviction that one *can* criticize them. A philosopher might conceivably claim to know, from considerations of physics or metaphysics, what are the constituents of the universe; on this ground, he might fault an historian for invoking entities which do not exist. (Witness the standard positivistic criticism of the *Zeitgeist* historians.) Alternatively, a logician, claiming to know what makes an inference valid, might criticize historians for employing invalid ones. Of course, the successful deployment of such arguments requires the assurance that the historical explanation in question has been properly understood; here historical knowledge seems indispensable. By the same token, the conclusions of this type of philosophy ought to be of interest to the historian in his own work. When the philosopher styles himself 'critical', the implication is not necessarily that he appoints himself as an authority with special licence to tell historians how to do history; the implication is, rather, that philosophers and historians can usefully engage in a critical exchange of arguments over issues of substantive interest to both.

A second question is: how does the critical approach differ from the speculative approach? The answer is far from obvious, since they are both committed, eventually, to raising ultimate questions which analytical philosophy excuses itself from raising. The difference is

13

largely one of method: instead of raising directly, say, the question of historical progress, the critical philosopher approaches the question obliquely, asking, first, whether the historical explanations actually employed allow for the notion of progress, and secondly, whether these explanations are so far justified. This oblique approach is not merely, as at first might appear, an intellectual detour, or 'beating about the bush'; rather it is a conscious application of Descartes's maxims, to the effect that large and unwieldy questions should be broken down into their component parts, and that simple questions should be tackled before complex ones. Speculative philosophy of history has long excited the imagination of nonspecialists by the impressive scope of its problems; this scope, however, has been bought at the price of a notorious vagueness which invites colorful turns of phrase rather than critical and reflective thought. The questions of whether history progresses and of whether the stuff of history is mental or material, are no doubt intriguing, but attempts at answering them in their original form have long been subject to the law of diminishing returns. Critical philosophy of history proceeds from the recognition that these questions are important, and need to be faced, but that they are unanswerable unless carefully analyzed into a number of more precise and specific questions, to be tackled in a piecemeal, step-by-step fashion.

The present essay is in this sense an essay in critical philosophy of history. It is my belief that philosophy evolves dialectically, through the sympathetic criticism of earlier thinkers. Philosophical criticism is never merely destructive in its intentions: there is usually no point criticizing a philosopher whom one considers to be *all* wrong; rather, one criticizes a philosopher for his errors in order to bring his true insights more sharply into focus. One obvious prerequisite for such criticism is that one considers the subject of criticism to be the bearer of important truths not otherwise available. This essay will take the form, in the main, of an exposition and a critical discussion of the views of the two foremost proponents of what I have called critical philosophy of history: Sir Karl R. Popper and R. G. Collingwood. Common to both is an insistence on the importance in historical research of viewing historical actions as rational responses to *problems*, and of analyzing the background of *tacit presuppositions* on which the problems have arisen – the method that Popper has labeled 'situational analysis'.

Because I intend to level major criticisms at both Popper and Collingwood, I wish to stress at the outset that I am fundamentally in sympathy with their general conception of historical method. The rationale for my own procedure in the present essay is this: the works of Popper and Collingwood have become integral parts of an intellectual tradition; even if we were able to scrap this tradition and start all over again from a *tabula rasa,* we would do so at the risk of a fatal impoverishment of our stock of thought. For someone interested in contributing to the elucidation of this particular approach to historical method, the sensible approach is to try to reconstruct the method from a critical appraisal of the foremost past contributors. This, in all modesty, is my present project.

The discussion will not, as some might expect, issue in the proposal of a comprehensive, independently argued, philosophical thesis. My procedure throughout will be critical and historical, not systematic-analytic. The reasons for this will, I hope, become clear in the course of the essay. Briefly, it is one of my conclusions that no comprehensive theory of historical method can be satisfactorily defended on purely logico-epistemological grounds; the defense of any such theory can be developed only in the course of substantive historical research. This, if true, is itself a philosophically significant conclusion. At the same time, it is a conclusion that points the way to interesting research programs in historiography; in the final chapter, I shall indicate some lines of research which I would consider relevant for the present purpose.

While I am not aiming to advance a comprehensive philosophical thesis, I am certainly prepared to defend a particular point of view; and, especially as I am assuming the role of a critic, I recognize the obligation to specify at the outset my point of view and the purpose of the criticism. Chapter 1 of this essay will be devoted to this purpose.

At this stage, my chief contention is that we do not know how to give a true account of historical method unless we know *precisely* what is wrong with the accounts given by Popper and Collingwood. Furthermore, we do not know what is wrong with Popper's theory of the historical understanding unless we view this theory in the light of his attempt to salvage his logic of scientific discovery from adverse criticisms advanced by the logical positivists; nor do we understand what is wrong with Collingwood's theory unless we understand his formulations as attempts to gain a hearing in the parochial atmosphere of Oxford philosophy in the thirties. Finally, although Collingwood is, chronologically, a predecessor of Popper, I do not think that the force of his position can be fully appreciated except in the perspective of the breakdown of Popper's program.

These considerations have determined the plan of this essay. Chapter 1 gives a preliminary outline of the 'Popper–Collingwood approach', and especially of the 'hard core' with which I find myself in agreement. Chapters 2 to 6 are devoted to a critical examination of Popper's program, noting how his theory of the historical understanding is formulated within the framework of his response to problems generated in the logic of science. The shortcomings of the program are revealed, e.g. in Popper's recent attempt to demarcate his own views from Collingwood's. Since Popper, in his later writings, bases his theory on certain notions derived from Gottlob Frege, the examination will have to involve a brief excursion into Frege's metaphysics. Chapters 7 to 10 examine Collingwood's theory of the historical understanding; the treatment is still critical, but the object of the criticism is to recast the theory into the most reasonable and most defensible form possible. Chapter 11 summarizes the main conclusions arrived at, and the Appendix illustrates the conclusions with an historical case study.

1. "The Popper-Collingwood Approach": Preliminary Outline

We commonly distinguish between two radically different types of explanation. One type of explanation consists in relating an event causally to one or more prior events, its so-called antecedent conditions. The relation between the event to be explained, the *explanandum,* and the event or events by which we explain it, the *explanans,* is expressed by a general, lawlike statement. We may explain an event causally either by assuming the lawlike statement to be known and pointing to the antecedent conditions, or by assuming the antecedent conditions to be known and pointing to the lawlike statement. The collapse of a steel bridge through metal fatigue might, for example, be explained to an engineer by citing the type and the amount of vibratory strain to which the bridge had been subjected, while to someone who has not heard of metal fatigue, it would be natural to explain the collapse by citing the generalization that all steel structures collapse when subjected to a particular kind of vibration over a specified period of time.

A different type of explanation consists in relating an action to the reasons for performing the action. Columbus's crossing of the Atlantic Ocean, for example, might be explained as an attempt to find a shorter sea route to the Far East. This explanation makes no mention of antecedent conditions, and it does not invoke any lawlike generalizations, but places the action within a unique context in which it is seen as a rational response to a problem. This type of explanation is called rational, as opposed to causal, explanation. So explained, Colombus's action presupposes a complex problem-situation. This problem-situation involves such problems as the distance from Spain to the Far East, the difficulties and perils of traveling that distance, and the expenses of customs along the way. These are problems from the vantage point of a particular motive, the

17

motive of achieving efficient and profitable trade with the Far East. In a rational explanation, these factors are not viewed as antecedent physical and economic conditions that caused Columbus to cross the Atlantic. In actual fact, as we know, the physical conditions were different from what Columbus thought; the eastward route was shorter and more effective than the westward route. Nor, on the other hand, do we achieve a satisfactory rational explanation by saying that Columbus thought the westward route was shorter. Columbus might have been deranged, in which case his thoughts would not be evidence of the rationality of his actions. (And, in fact, his conviction on this score does appear as something in the nature of an obsession.) But if we accept that it was reasonable for Columbus to hold that belief, then we can see his voyage as a rational response to the problem-situation. And if we accept the motive – to facilitate the Eastern trade – as a rational one and not merely as an arbitrary whim, then we can see the entire problem-situation as a rational one, that is, one in which we are able to involve ourselves intellectually.

Columbus's voyage may also be explained causally. A Marxist might explain Columbus as the blind instrument of nascent capitalism in need of cheap raw materials. A psychoanalyst might explain his voyage as over-compensation of an inferiority complex. In both cases, the logical relation between the problem-situation and Columbus's solution becomes irrelevant. To the Marxist, it is just an accident that America was discovered by someone who thought he was on his way to India; if it hadn't been Columbus, it would have been someone else. The economic necessities of capitalism required that *someone* traveled to America, for no matter what reason. To the psychoanalyst, Columbus's reasons for his voyage are mere self-deception, conjured up to conceal his shameful, unconscious motives. In general, when we explain an historical event causally, we refuse to view the behavior of the agents as human *actions,* of the kind that we ourselves are conscious of performing. When we ourselves act, we think we have reasons for our actions, and we think that knowledge of these reasons is essential for understanding our actions. When we explain other people's behavior by reference to causes, and not to reasons, we remove it from the sphere of human action as we know it from our own conscious experience.

It is of the essence of the 'Popper–Collingwood approach' to historical understanding that historical events should be explained rationally, not causally. According to both Popper and Collingwood, an historical action must be understood as the attempt to solve a problem, a problem which the historian must reconstruct from a background network of tacit presuppositions. These presuppositions are not necessarily in the agent's mind, consciously or subconsciously, and they cannot be retrieved by a kind of historical psychoanalysis. If the presuppositions are to present the problem as a real problem, and hence make the agent's solution intelligible to us, they must be the kind of presuppositions which it would be reasonable for the agent to make in the historical situation in which he found himself.

This methodological rule: 'Always seek rational, rather than causal, explanations', may be viewed either as a very bold conception or as a severe limitation on the study of history. On the assumption that most historical events cannot be rationally understood in the manner described, the Popper–Collingwood approach would seem to contain a large measure of skepticism toward historical knowledge. It is commonly held, for instance, that we cannot really penetrate the thought-structures of past centuries, that medieval and ancient peoples had a rationality, or even a logic, radically different from ours, and that we cannot, therefore, hope fully to understand them; all we can do is record their behavior and the events that befell them. If this assumption is granted, the restriction of historical explanation to rational explanations would indeed mean a severe restriction of the scope of historical research. But I do not think that either Popper or Collingwood would grant this assumption. Collingwood held it as 'a point of honor' always to try to understand other people's unexpressed presuppositons when they were different from his own. Popper has repeatedly ridiculed the 'myth' that people need a common framework of shared assumptions in order to understand each other. Both, it seems, are deeply committed to the view that there is one and only one common human rationality, and that the presuppositions of alien people, past or present, are always in principle intelligible, given sufficient imagination, patience, and goodwill.

I regard this as one of the most essential features of the Popper–Collingwood approach. The rejection of causal explanations of human affairs is today something of a commonplace. Especially in Germany and in Scandinavia, there has lately emerged a superficial and irresponsible antipositivism, which exploits this rejection of causal explanations as an excuse for rejecting wholesale the categories of both rationality and objectivity. As a consequence, anything goes. The very notion of 'fact', for instance, is frequently said to belong to the limited rationality of the bourgeoisie, which is bent on objectifying and manipulating society, while the class-conscious proletariat has its own rationality, inaccessible to the bourgeoisie. I shall not bore the reader with a thoroughgoing analysis of this particular tedium; I only wish to stress the potentially disastrous consequences of holding that one can understand only those presuppositional frameworks which one shares oneself. Such a view involves that one is accountable only to those with whom one is in fundamental agreement, with the consequence that all fundamental issues are excluded from the sphere of rational discussion. While the rationalism of Popper or Collingwood is admittedly very bold, the alternative view seems to me utterly unacceptable, intellectually and morally.

Once this has been said, it may be necessary to explain why in the present essay I direct most of my critical arguments *against* Popper and Collingwood. Many of the criticisms are detailed and technical, and it may be necessary at the outset to indicate the point of these criticisms by summarizing the main shortcomings of these two thinkers and explaining why these shortcomings are worthy of notice.

The present-day attack on rationality in the human sciences has chiefly taken the form of identifying the cause of rationality with the hypothetico-deductive method and then triumphantly showing that the hypothetico-deductive method cannot be applied to human affairs. Popper is an almost passionate advocate of rationality, one of the few who has the courage to call himself a rationalist in an age where this word is mostly used as a term of abuse. None the less, Popper actually aids his opponents by reinforcing the identification of rationality with the hypothetico-deductive method. I think Popper is quite right in characterizing rationality as the attitude of accepting, and even actively seeking, refutations of one's own beliefs. But I think Popper is wrong in taking the role of crucial experiments in science as a paradigm of this attitude, and in demanding that all rational research must conform to the hypothetico-deductive pattern found in natural science. My arguments against Popper on this count are chiefly of two kinds.

In the first place, the natural-scientific method, in Popper's own analysis, is not characterized solely by rationality and open-mindedness, but at least as much by dogmatism. Crucial experiments by which scientists refute theories are not crucial unless the scientists treat the observation-statements as irrefutable; yet Popper has offered no reason why these statements should be regarded as less fallible than theories. In fact, he asserts explicitly that they are not. Crucial experiments, on Popper's showing, are based on conventions to the effect of treating the observation-statements as irrefutable, at least for the duration of each experiment. This concession to dogmatism seriously undermines the case for treating the natural-scientific method as paradigmatic of the open-minded attitude.

In the second place, Popper does not make a convincing case for extending the hypothetico-deductive method from the natural to the human sciences. It is essential to the hypothetico-deductive method that one can effectively distinguish between a theoretical and a factual level of discourse. Falsification comes about when a theory is contradicted by a factual statement, and this is impossible unless we can effectively distinguish between two classes of statements, theoretical and factual. The 'factual' level may be thought to be just a lower level of theorizing, but the essential thing is the distinctness of the two levels. Now it is Popper's view, which I wholeheartedly share, that human thoughts are to be historically reconstructed, not as psychological processes, but as logical chains of reasoning. But this reconstruction requires that the thoughts of historical agents are thought through by the historian himself, and so incorporated into his own theorizing. As a consequence, the distinction between the theoretical and the factual level collapses, and falsification by crucial experiment is ruled out. Popper sees this discrepancy and tackles it by flatly denying that the historian has to think through the thoughts he attempts to reconstruct. I think this claim is obviously erroneous, and I intend to show that Popper gets into a hopeless tangle when trying to defend it.

Collingwood's possibly greatest merit lies in his having fully realized the implications of this coalescence of the thoughts of historical agents with the thoughts of the historian. The reason why I cannot wholeheartedly accept Collingwood's theory is that it is vulnerable in other, equally important, respects. One particularly sinister aspect of the present-day revolt against reason is the rejection of formal logic. This rejection takes several forms. It is frequently claimed that, since formal logic is based on relations between declarative statements, it follows that it is concerned only with the descriptive use of language characteristic of natural science, and that the human sciences, which involve different uses of language, require a different logic. Another line, which is defended even by some highly distinguished logicians, is that logic is merely a description of the most general features of our conceptual scheme, and that other people, in different places and ages, may have different conceptual schemes and different logics. Both claims are irrefutable and self-refuting since they make absolutely no sense except on the presupposition that both speaker and hearer accept the laws of formal logic. It is tacitly understood, for instance, that the speaker does not wish to contradict himself, that he wishes to assert the truth of a statement that validly follows from a true statement, etc.

In his later writings Collingwood lends support to both these non-sensical claims by presenting his analysis of presuppositions as a new logic which is to replace formal logic. Collingwood's arguments and examples make it fairly clear that he confuses logic with semantics and semantics with hermeneutics. I shall argue that his rejection of formal logic is more a matter of unhappy formulation that anything else and I believe it is possible to re-formulate his theory without any absurd consequences. The consequences of his own formulations are, however, so serious that I find it necessary to take strong exception to some of the formulations and to invest a considerable effort in dis-entangling the various strands of his argumentation.

These criticisms will be argued in considerable detail. I hope this brief outline will suffice to provide a focus for the purpose and direction of the more detailed and technical arguments to follow.

2. Popper's Program in the Logic of Science

Central to Popper's theory of scientific method is the idea of *progress* or *growth of knowledge;* and his controversial demarcation criterion can usefully be viewed as a criterion of scientific progress. But this progress, according to Popper, cannot be viewed as an accumulation of truths since we do not and cannot have any criterion of truth. All knowledge is conjectural and it progresses through the elimination of errors and the consequent approximation towards truth. Believing that Tarski showed that the concept of 'truth' is meaningful, although it carries no criteria for its own application, Popper has expended a great deal of effort on showing that the concept of 'truthlikeness' or 'approximation to the truth' is meaningful, although once again we have no criteria for such approximation. The concept of 'truthlikeness' is plainly meant to provide an epistemological interpretation of his methodological concept of 'progress'. What Popper does not seem to have noticed, although it has been pointed out to him by Imre Lakatos,[1] is that since the concept of progress is linked to methodological criteria, while the concept of truthlikeness is not, the two remain conceptually unconnected and the epistemological interpretation of progress remains an open problem in Popper's philosophy. The problem of the epistemological interpretation of progress is indeed the central problem in Popper's philosophy. On the one hand Popper is an anti-relativist and cannot afford to leave the concept of progress as a purely methodologically – i.e. conventionally – defined concept; on the other hand he is a fallibilist, and cannot afford the apriorism implicit in defining progress by means of truthlikeness, thereby investing the latter concept with criteria for its application.

The development of Popper's philosophy, I wish to suggest, is something like this: In his first book *Logik der Forschung* Popper was not troubled by the epistemological interpretation of progress since he had not yet become acquainted with Tarski's concept of truth; the problem of that book was merely the problem of finding a criterion of progress. An attempted logical criterion failed and had to be qualified by a reference to historical circumstances, specifically, the historically ascertained consensus of the scientific community. At this stage Popper remained content with a historically relative logical criterion of progress. The idea that the rationality of scientific decisions depends on historical circumstances provided a powerful positive heuristic for the philosophy of history and seems to have inspired Popper's awareness of the explanatory (or 'explicatory') value of problem-situations and of networks of tacit assumptions – the guiding idea in Popper's situational analysis as developed e.g. in *The Poverty of Historicism* and *Conjectures and Refutations*. However, once Popper had accepted Tarski's concept of truth he grew aware of the need for an epistemological interpretation of his methodological concept of progress. At the same time his preoccupations with social philosophy made him acutely sensitive to the dangers of historical relativism, a sensitivity manifested in *The Open Society and its Enemies*. These concerns led him to develop the concept of truthlikeness, buttressed with a quasi-Fregean metaphysics. This gambit, I shall argue, did not resolve the dilemma of relativism versus apriorism, but it did undermine the positive heuristic of his earlier approach. This is not to say that Popper ought to have embraced relativism, only that his rejection of relativism, in the precise form that it took, did not solve the problems which led him to relativism in the first place.

Popper's idea of scientific method as set forth in *Logik der Forschung* (1934) incorporates three main theses: the thesis of falsifiability, the thesis of fallibility, and the thesis of conventionalism. Commentators and critics have not always been aware of the presence of all three of these, but have more often than not paid attention exclusively to the thesis of falsifiability. This has had the effect of precluding, to a not inconsiderable extent, fruitful discussion of the problems arising from the conjunction of these three theses.

The thesis of falsifiability depends upon the following logical nicety:

My proposal is based on an *asymmetry* between verifiability and falsifiability; an asymmetry which results from the logical form of universal statements. For these are never derivable from singular statements, but can be contradicted by singular statements. Consequently, it is possible by means of purely deductive inferences (with the help of the *modus tollens* of classical logic) to argue from the truth of singular statements to the falsity of universal statements.[2]

This, we shall note, is so far a purely logical claim. Let p be a universal statement and q a singular statement; *given* the conditional 'if p then q', we are perfectly justified in concluding from not-q to not-p, although we are not justified in concluding from q to p. This *logical* asymmetry is not controversial, but is trivially entailed by the principle of *modus tollens*. On the other hand, it does not by itself carry any methodological implications.

The next step is of greater consequence. The class of spatio-temporal singular statements is postulated as the class of basic statements, in an as yet unspecified sense of 'basic'. The class of those basic statements which contradict a given universal statement is called the class of its 'potential falsifiers'. These assumptions permit the formulation of the thesis of falsifiability: A theory is 'falsifiable' or 'scientific' if, and only if, the class of its potential falsifiers is not empty.[3] The theory is falsified if a single one of its potential falsifiers is corroborated; the theory is corroborated by degrees proportionate to the falsification of its potential falsifiers. The 'empirical content' of the theory is defined as the class of its potential falsifiers. We can now give a preliminary sketch of Popper's idea of scientific method: The growth of scientific knowledge consists in the progressive replacement of falsified theories by new theories with increased corroboration and increased empirical content. To the extent that scientific knowledge is regarded as paradigmatic for the growth of knowledge in general, this idea yields, as a corollary, a general code of intellectual honesty, in the requirement that we lay all our theories open to criticism and refutation, by unambiguously specifying the classes of their potential falsifiers.

The story, in fact, is not quite so simple. I have not yet specified the sense in which Popper designates spatio-temporal singular statements as 'basic'. If Popper had held that these statements are basic by virtue of their truth being immediately given in sense-experience, he would have laid himself open to the criticism leveled at him by, for example, Ayer, in *Language, Truth and Logic*. Ayer argues that no statement ever expresses a 'bare fact'; in saying that a particular fact conflicts with a theory, we are *eo ipso* asserting one more hypothesis, which is as fallible as the theory which we set out to test. In the case of a negative experiment, the scientist has to decide whether to regard the theory itself, or one or more auxiliary hypotheses, as falsified. When Ayer concludes, 'Logically, our freedom is unlimited',[4] he is no doubt right, as long as the emphasis is on the word 'logically'; where he is wrong is in believing that he is thereby criticizing Popper. (In this, Ayer was, incidentally, following in the footsteps of Neurath.[5]) Popper, in fact, insisted that there is no rock bottom of knowledge, and that 'statements can be justified only by statements'.[6] Accordingly, he argued vigorously against the alleged 'psychologism' of Carnap and Neurath, both of whom held, at one point, that basic statements are psychologically immediate, and hence incorrigible. *Our* subjective certainty, Popper argued, in no way guarantees the truth of any statement in a manner relevant to the testing of scientific theories.[7] These are the considerations which underlie what I call Popper's thesis of fallibility: No matter what certainty *we* may possess, all *statements* are equally fallible.

This second thesis affects the first in the following manner: The postulate of a class of basic statements does not, in itself, permit a straightforward methodological interpretation of the logical asymmetry entailed by the *modus tollens*. The deductive inferences involved in scientific testing are not simply of the form 'if p then q', but rather 'if p and r, then q', where r is the auxiliary hypothesis which permits us to regard q as basic relative to p. *Modus tollens* permits us to conclude from not-q either to not-p or to not-r, but *modus tollens* does not tell us to which. Logically, our choice is unlimited, to quote Ayer once more. It is evident, therefore, that the thesis of fallibilism calls for an amendment of the thesis of falsifiability.

This is precisely what Popper sought to achieve by proposing a third thesis, the thesis of conventionalism. According to this thesis, basic statements are 'basic' by virtue of a methodological decision, i.e. an agreement among scientists to treat these statements as basic relative to the theory which is at the time being called in question and put to the test: 'From a logical point of view, the testing of a theory depends upon basic statements whose acceptance or rejection, in its turn, depends upon our *decisions*. Thus it is *decisions* which settle the fate of theories.'[8] Calling a class of singular statements 'basic' implies no more than the recognition that they are, by mutual agreement among scientists, treated as unproblematic, for the time being. No one statement is in principle sacrosanct: whenever a currently 'basic' statement becomes suspect, the methodological decision may be reversed, and the statement put to the test. The basic statements do not, therefore, form any kind of rock bottom of knowledge:

> Science does not rest upon solid bedrock. The bold structure of its theories rises, as it were, above a swamp. It is like a building erected on piles. The piles are driven down from above into the swamp, but not down to any natural or 'given' base; and if we stop driving the piles deeper, it is not because we have reached firm ground. We simply stop when we are satisfied that the piles are firm enough to carry the structure, at least for the time being.[9]

It is important here to distinguish two claims, one innocent and one highly risky. The phrase 'we have not reached firm ground' may seem to convey the wholly uncontroversial idea of the open-endedness of the process of scientific inquiry. But there is a much more dangerous claim involved here. According to the thesis of falsifiability, the process of inquiry, though open-ended, is nonetheless *progressive:* it progresses through error elimination. Now the thesis of conventionalism tells us that the *criteria* for error elimination, and hence for progress, are themselves open to change by fiat. To see the problem, one has only to ponder the force of the rider 'for the time being'. If a certain class of statements are, at any one time, acknowledged as 'basic', what could ever make us reverse this decision? For the methodological decision to be reversed, at least one basic statement would have to become 'problematic', but the only criterion so far offered for regarding a statement as 'problematic' is inconsistency with a basic statement. Barring internal inconsistency among the basic statements, there seems to be no criterion whereby a basic statement may be called in question, and so the criteria for scientific progress are inescapably and exclusively conventional.

It is easy to see how this position must prove troublesome from the point of view of Popper's later acceptance of the correspondence theory of truth. By adopting this conventionalism with regard to the basic statements, Popper has in effect — though tacitly — precluded any interpretation of the scientific method in terms of a realist epistemology or a correspondence theory of truth. Popper himself would deny this: the basic statements are not 'true by convention', but merely exempt from testing; their truth still depends on correspondence with facts. But this will not do: if the conventions do not license us to regard the basic statements as true, then the latter will never have the force required to falsify any theory, in any epistemological sense of 'falsify'. The *modus tollens* permits us to conclude from the truth of a singular statement to the falsity of a universal statement, but from the conventional acceptance of a singular statement, we can conclude, at most, to the conventional rejection of a universal statement. Science, so conceived, is a purely self-contained game, which not only lacks an epistemological interpretation, but which effectively prohibits such interpretation — unless one is prepared to admit into one's epistemology some structural equivalent of the methodological decision, something like 'hard facts' or 'first principles', or some other rock bottom of knowledge. This Popper has, understandably, been unwilling to do.

Yet Popper's conventionalism never entailed that scientific decisions are arbitrary; science may be just a game, but it is a *rule-governed* game. We do not make or break conventions at will; we *inherit* a set of conventions, and with it a complex problem-situation, with the scientific tradition which we take over from our predecessors. Scientific decisions are not just whims; they are rational decisions; not, however, timelessly rational, but rational in relation to a specific problem-situation, i.e. rational in relation to their historical preconditions. In *Logik der Forschung* this important corollary of the thesis of conventionalism is barely hinted at, in a brief discussion of the undesirability of proposing 'metaphysical' theories, which lack currently testable consequences: 'a link with the science of the day is as a rule established only by those theories which are proposed in an attempt to meet the current problem-situation; that is, the current difficulties, contradictions, and falsifications.'[10] Later, however, in *Conjectures and Refutations* (1962), this point is reiterated with all desirable explicitness:

Without any knowledge of the results of Galileo and Kepler, of the problems that were resolved by these results, and of Newton's problem of explaining Galileo's and Kepler's solutions by a unified theory, we should find Newton's theory just as much beyond discussion as any metaphysical theory. In other words every *rational* theory, no matter whether scientific or philosophical, is rational in so far as it tries to *solve certain problems*. A theory is comprehensible and reasonable only in its relation to a given *problem-situation*, and it can be rationally discussed only by discussing this relation.[11]

Popper's early philosophy of science, as I have presented it, has clearly skeptical implications. The dependence on problem-situations, and hence on historical traditions, incurs the liability (from Popper's point of view) of historical relativism, while salvaging the theory from the outright irrationalism which would otherwise seem unavoidable. At the same time, the introduction of problem-situations marks a substantive problem-shift in Popper's philosophy: the role of problem-situations, and of 'unproblematic background knowledge' in historical explanation moves into the focus of interest. In this way, the conventionalist gambit, makeshift and unsatisfactory from the point of view of the philosophy of science, provides a positive heuristic for the philosophy of history.

3. The Fruitfulness of Historicism

Despite its title, *The Poverty of Historicism* (1944–45; 1957) is *not* a critique of historicism, if we take that word in its ordinary sense, as referring to the relativistic views associated with, for instance, Croce or Dilthey. Popper employs the term 'historicism' as a technical term, which is explained as follows:

> I mean by 'historicism' an approach to the social sciences which assumes that *historical prediction* is their principal aim, and which assumes that this aim is attainable by discovering the 'rhythms' or the 'patterns', the 'laws' or the 'trends' that underlie the evolution of history.[1]

It is reasonably clear that Popper wants this description to apply to practically all thinkers of Marxist or Hegelian leanings; it is equally clear, however, that it does, in fact, apply only to strict historical determinists, such as Engels, Kautsky, Plekhanov, and very few others.

While Popper appropriates the term 'historicism' for what is ordinarily called 'historical determinism', he coins the novel term 'historism' (adapted from the German *Historismus*) to replace 'historicism' in its ordinary sense. This term is introduced in *The Open Society and its Enemies* (1945): 'A theory of this kind which emphasizes the sociological dependence of our opinions is sometimes called *sociologism;* if the historical dependence is emphasized, it is called *historism.*'[2] (Since Popper sometimes claims that the word 'historicism' is his own innovation it may be pointed out that as early as 1938, Maurice Mandelbaum used this term as the English equivalent of *Historismus*.)[3] As I see no particular advantages in Popper's nomenclature, I intend to use the word 'historicism' in its commonly accepted meaning.

This meaning, already hinted at in Popper's explication of 'historism', is made abundantly clear by Mandelbaum, who deserves quoting at some length:

> This view of the world may express itself in many variant forms. Perhaps the most common is that which holds every set of cultural values to be relative to the age in which it is dominant. This form of historicism, which we may best speak of as the historicity of values, is often identified with historicism as such. However, there is also a prevalent form of historicism which we may call that of knowledge, and it is with this form that we are here dealing. With respect to knowledge, historicism claims that no statement can be considered true or false without reference to the time at which it was formulated; for it, like every other entity, must be understood in the light of the ever-changing process of history. *Although this view has long been given up with reference to such statements as the natural scientist makes,* it is still held to apply to historical accounts. (My italics)[4]

The italicized clause strikes a note of irony: this was written only four years after Popper had committed himself to just such a view concerning the natural sciences. The overthrow of a scientific theory presupposes the acceptance of basic statements, an acceptance which is founded on nothing but a decision, and so is historically dependent.

The sociological and historical dependence of scientific discoveries has also been made quite explicit by Popper:

> All this means that a young scientist who hopes to make discoveries is badly advised if his teacher tells him, 'Go round and observe,' and that he is well advised if his teacher tells him: 'Try to learn what people are discussing nowadays in science. Find out where difficulties arise, and take an interest in disagreements. These are the questions which you should take up.' In other words, you should study the *problem situation* of the day.[5]

Now all that is here admitted is the historical dependence of the *questions* which a scientist may profitably ask; Popper has never admitted that the *answers* are similarly dependent. Yet this is an inevitable corollary of the thesis of conventionalism: while the possible range of questions is determined by the problem-situation, the possible

31

range of answers is determined by the basic statements, i.e. the class of those singular statements which are not, at the time, considered problematic. If that which is problematic (the problem-situation) is historically dependent, then it follows trivially that the residual class, that which is not problematic (the basic statements), is historically dependent as well.

In charging Popper's early philosophy of science with historical relativism, or 'historicism', in its ordinary sense, I am conscious of my obligation to meet Popper's own anti-relativist arguments, since these are based, in part, precisely on his idea of scientific method. Let us consider, therefore, Popper's argument against the sociology of knowledge in *The Open Society*. (Sociologism and historicism differ only in matters of emphasis; the relativism is common to both.) The argument is based on the contention that the proponents of sociologism have proved, at most, the impossibility of objectivity as a subjective attitude, while the possibility of reaching objective truth, despite biased attitudes, remains untouched. 'The sociology of knowledge is not only self-destructive, not only a rather gratifying object of socio-analysis, it also shows an astounding failure to understand its main subject, the *social aspects of knowledge*, or rather, of scientific method.'[6] The point is that the objectivity of science is not an individual habit of mind, but resides in the exchange of criticism within the scientific community: 'ironically enough, objectivity is closely bound up with the *social aspect of scientific method,* with the fact that science and scientific objectivity do not (and cannot) result from the attempts of an individual scientist to be "objective", but from the *friendly-hostile co-operation of many scientists.*'[7] So, in the first place, scientific knowledge is intersubjective knowledge, and cannot, for that reason, be tainted by individual prejudices. But, as Popper is well aware, intersubjectivity is not objectivity: there is, *prima facie*, nothing to prevent the entire scientific community from being blinded by prejudices built into a particular social arrangement or a particular historical epoch. It is indeed the central contention of the sociology of science, as represented for instance by Kuhn,[8] that this is precisely what happens. So the existence of a scientific community is not in itself a guarantee of objectivity; there is, in the second place, a need for external checks on the scientific community. Popper approaches this subject in a curiously roundabout manner:

Secondly, scientists try to avoid talking at cross-purposes. . . . In the natural sciences this is achieved by recognizing experience as the impartial arbiter of their controversies. When speaking of 'experience' I have in mind experience of a 'public' character, like observations, and experiments, as opposed to experience in the sense of more 'private' aesthetic or religious experience; and an experience is 'public' if everybody who takes the trouble can repeat it.[9]

I think Popper here illegitimately smuggles in the words 'impartial arbiter'; fully aware that the objectivity of science requires experience as an impartial arbiter, he speaks as though this role could be filled by any experience which is public and repeatable, i.e. intersubjective. For Popper's methodology of science admits of no other 'experience' than the socially defined, intersubjective experience furnished by the conventional acceptance of basic statements. Scientific theories, in Popper's own view, cannot clash with facts; they can clash only with singular statements, and the falsifying force of singular statements is due entirely to a scientific *decision*. The conventional acceptance of basic statements does, of course, guarantee the public and intersubjective nature of scientific knowledge, but it does not do this by appealing to experience as an impartial arbiter, in the sense of an objective, external check, transcending the merely intersubjective. Yet something of this sort seems to be required for the refutation of sociologism, and Popper's otherwise inexplicable use of the words 'impartial arbiter' suggests that he himself has not been entirely unaware of the fact.

Popper's later offensive against the conventionalist roots of relativism will be considered in due course; for the moment, I have been concerned to argue that this relativism is implicit in his early philosophy. The main point I wish to make in this section is this: once one acknowledges – rightly or wrongly – the historical relativity of scientific knowledge, this acknowledgement has far-reaching implications for one's understanding of historical knowledge. Scientific knowledge depends on scientific decisions, and a scientific decision is an historical event. Just as scientific decisions have to be judged in relation to an historical background, so any historical event must be judged in relation to its particular background. This implies that historical explanations are, in a sense, *sui generis*: historical events cannot be explained in the same way as natural events, by appeal to general causal laws; each historical event has to be rendered intelligible in relation to the complex problem-situation from which it arose. I think that this approach to historical explanation, the method of situational analysis, is a natural consequence of historicism, but I have no wish to suggest that the converse is also the case. A non-relativistic argument for the *sui generis* nature of historical explanation may be made by an appeal to a principle of continuity in the history of thought; I shall argue later that Collingwood makes a particularly forceful case for a view of this kind.

In saying that historical explanations are *sui generis,* what is it that is being denied? In the Introduction, I mentioned Hempel's thesis, according to which historical explanations are ordinary causal explanations, and causal explanations have the form of deductive inferences. That is, an historian explains an event E by relating it to a finite number of other events, which form its necessary and sufficient conditions C, as specified in a general law. The point of advancing such a thesis, obviously, is to affirm an essential unity of method between the natural and the human sciences. The Hempel thesis has long been argued to death, and it is no part of my purpose to revive this particular argument, but the most obvious criticism of it ought to be noted. The difficulty is that historians do not *seem* to employ general laws; as a rule, they seem to infer the explanandum nondeductively, from a particular event or from a finite collection of particular events. Hempel's answer has been that the general law which warrants the inference has been implicitly presupposed, and Popper has argued that the general laws employed by historians are, as a rule, so trivial as not to require explicit statement. To take one of Popper's examples: When we explain Giordano Bruno's death by pointing to the fact of his being burnt at the stake, we are tacitly assuming the general law that 'all living things die when exposed to intense heat'.[10] We need not mention the law in the explanation, because of its evident triviality. However, the triviality of the 'law' is not only a good reason for not mentioning it; it is an equally good reason for not considering it a part of the explanation. For the truth of the law that 'all living things die when exposed to intense heat' is neither more nor less questionable than the validity of inferring Bruno's death from the fact of his being burnt at the stake. If there was a problem with the original nondeductive inference, then that problem is now reproduced in the major premise. Furthermore, there

34

is no a priori reason why we should not regard the deductive inference as equally problematic, and assert that it stands in need of a further major premise: 'If all living things die when exposed to extreme heat, and if Bruno was burnt at the stake, then Bruno died', and so forth *ad infinitum*. This is the standard criticism of the Hempel thesis, originally advanced, I believe, by Alan Donagan.[11]

In *The Poverty of Historicism* Popper endorses the Hempel thesis, and in *The Open Society* he also claims the questionable honor of having been the first to propound this thesis, in his definition of causality in *Logik der Forschung*.[12] Be that as it may, in *The Poverty of Historicism*, Popper is already plainly aware of the heuristic poverty of deductivism, and whatever is cf interest in this book owes nothing to the deductive thesis. Justly famous is the *reductio ad absurdum* of the idea of historical prediction. If it is granted that the course of social events is, to any extent at all, influenced by the changing states of human knowledge, then, in order to predict future social events, we should have to predict the future state of our knowledge; otherwise we should have an uncontrolled variable, which might upset the whole prediction. But the prediction of future knowledge is a logical impossibility. In order to predict, say, a future scientific discovery, we should actually have to make that discovery now, otherwise we could not know what the discovery would be like. But then we would not be predicting future knowledge, but ascertaining present knowledge, and the future would be as much in the dark as ever. It is worth noting that this unpredictability thesis is not linked to a free-will thesis: it is not because we have a free will (though Popper believes that we do) that we are unpredictable, but, on the contrary, because our intentions are constantly frustrated and defeated by the logic of social situations; here, the situation of making social predictions. In general, Popper argues, human affairs tend to turn out differently from what was intended, because human intentions are constrained, and thus imperfectly realized, by the logic of social situations. Popper's favorite example is from the sphere of economic action. A man who wishes to buy a house in a small village is normally not interested in raising the prices of houses in that village; yet his entry into this limited market will automatically have the effect of raising prices. Likewise, in the political sphere, a revolution always generates a counter-revolution because of the special interests vested in the *status quo*. These ideas are certainly not novel: Adam Smith introduced the idea of the 'invisible hand' in the economy, Edmund Burke pointed to the role of vested interests in politics, and they both served as sources for Hegel's notion of the 'cunning of reason'. The point is that notions such as these do not fit into the deductive model of explanation; explaining an event by invoking the logic of the situation is something very different from invoking a set of necessary and sufficient conditions. The market, for instance, is neither an event nor a thing; nor can it be adequately explained as a finite collection of either. Now one can formulate laws governing the behavior of the market, and one may conceivably also formulate general laws governing the behavior of vested interests in politics (although no one has yet done this), but it would be odd to say that we 'explain' an event by deriving it from such laws together with antecedent conditions. We do not explain a social event by relating it causally to its antecedent conditons; we explain it by relating it rationally to the complex situation in which it took place. For that, we do not need general laws, nor will general laws be any help, unless they refer to complex situations, such as the market. So it is not the generality of the law that matters, but its reference to the social situation in which the event took place.

In *The Poverty of Historicism*, these implications are imperfectly realized. In the suggestive chapter 'Situational Logic in History', Popper castigates Tolstoy for believing that the course of history is determined by such things as the 'spirit' of an age, or of a people, or of an army. But, while Popper expresses his contempt for such 'spirits', he grants that they are not altogether redundant in historical explanation; they indicate something that is missing from the simple deductive model:

I feel that they indicate, at least, the existence of a lacuna, of a place which it is the task of sociology to fill with something more sensible, such as an analysis of problems arising within a tradition. There is room for a more detailed analysis of the *logic of stituations*.[13]

Having arrived at this important insight, Popper attempts, however, to squeeze it into the deductive model. Two things are needed, he suggests. In the first place, there is a need for analytical 'models of political situations as well as of social movements such as scientific and industrial progress';[14] in the second place, there is a need to 'introduce a preconceived selective point of view into one's history'.[15] Once the significance of the logic of situations is recognized, these suggestions appear strikingly irrelevant: what is needed is not for the historian to bring analytical models *to* the study of history, but to recognize the traditions, problems, and problem-situations to be found *in* history. Likewise, a *preconceived* point of view is valueless in this context; what matters is the recognition that there is one and only one point of view appropriate to each historical event.

This is implicitly recognized by Popper in the following chapter, 'The Institutional Theory of Progress', where he addresses himself to the analysis of the effects of institutions on the progress of science. What Popper does in this chapter is to actually outline an explanation of scientific progress, noting the institutional conditions for the emergence and the survival of a scientific tradition. Now institutions are something that actually exist, something that the historian discovers in the course of his research; they are not merely analytical tools which the historian brings to the material. At the same time, Popper notes, the institutional conditions for scientific progress are neither necessary nor sufficient conditions; science may prosper under the most repressive institutions, and it may stagnate under the most liberal ones. So the explanation of scientific progress in terms of institutional frameworks is not a causal explanation in the deductivist sense of 'cause' as necessary and sufficient conditions.

A similar instance of Popper's application of situational analysis is the explanation of Plato's reaction against the open society, in the book entitled *The Open Society*. Popper has frequently been accused of the anachronism of calling Plato a 'totalitarian party politician'. But what Popper in fact says is that such an interpretation *seems to* be consistent with the available evidence, and in the very next sentence he goes on: 'But one only has to put the matter in this blunt fashion in order to feel that there is something seriously amiss with this interpretation. At any rate, so I felt, when I had formulated it.'[16] The difficulty is that, although Plato formulates a seemingly totalitarian plan for social organization, yet he occasionally expresses an apparently sincere hatred of tyranny. This sentiment is not wholly consistent with the presentation of Plato as *just* a power-hungry party politician. Popper is ready to ascribe genuinely humanitarian motives to Plato, but the ascription of such motives requires a particular background, or problem-situation, against which it makes sense to construe Plato's political program as an expression of humanitarianism. This Popper finds in what he calls 'the strain of civilization', a social and cultural malaise incurred by the rapid transition of the city-state from a 'closed' tribal society, protected by a mythical tradition, to an 'open' democratic society, informed and made insecure by a critical and scientific tradition.

> I believe that Plato, with deep sociological insight, found that his contemporaries were suffering under a severe strain, and that this strain was due to the social revolution which had begun with the rise of democracy and individualism. He succeeded in discovering the main causes of their deeply rooted unhappiness — social change, and social dissension – and he did his utmost to fight them.[17]

Plato's political program is explained, then, as an intelligible reaction to a social strain; evidently this is something radically different from 'explaining' the event by relating it causally to its necessary and sufficient conditions.

This idea of historical method as the method of rendering an event intelligible by relating it to a problem-situation is, as I have suggested, traceable to Popper's early realization that scientific decisions are rational only in relation to the current problem-situation in science. It has proved one of the most fruitful ideas in Popper's philosophy. Apart from the use made of it by Popper himself – notably in his studies of the early Greeks – it has provided a powerful source of inspiration for men who have learnt from Popper: Gombrich in the history of art, Agassi in the history of science, and Gallie in the philosophy of history. Yet so long as Popper had not come to terms with the problem of relativism in the philosophy of science, he did not venture to assert the actual existence of problem-situations in history, fearing, I suppose, that such an assertion would commit him to the very moral relativism which, in *The Open Society*, he was concerned to combat. In this book, therefore, problem-situations are described merely as interpretative models, or preconceived points of view, brought by the historian to his research. Later, after developing his calculus of verisimilitude, Popper became convinced, rightly or wrongly, that he had solved the problem of historical relativism, a conviction which brought about a new problem-shift in Popper's philosophy, with new implications for the philosophy of history.

4. From History to Metaphysics

In 1961, *The Open Society* was re-issued with a new addendum by the author. Here Popper attempts a refutation of relativism, based on the notion that scientific progress consists in getting nearer to the truth – the notion of 'truthlikeness' or 'verisimilitude'.

> The main philosophical malady of our time is an intellectual and moral relativism, the latter being at least in part based upon the former. ... In this *addendum* I shall first suggest that a dose of Tarski's theory of truth, stiffened perhaps by my own theory of getting nearer to the truth, may go a long way towards curing this malady ...[1]

Tarski's theory of truth cannot be reviewed here; I shall merely note what, according to Popper, are its salient features, with the general *caveat* that there is controversy as to whether Tarski's results can really be interpreted in this manner. In the first place, as Popper sees it, Tarski's semantic definition of truth involves the rehabilitation of the concept of 'truth' as 'correspondence with facts': 'In my opinion, *it is not his successful description of a method for defining "true"* which makes Tarski's work philosophically so important, but his *rehabilitation of the correspondence theory of truth* ...'[2] In the second place, Tarski not only defined truth as correspondence with facts without appealing to a criterion of truth; he actually proved that no such criterion is available: 'One immediate result of Tarski's work on truth is the following theorem of logic: *there can be no general criterion of truth.*'[3] In short, we can quite meaningfully talk about 'truth' without pretending to have a criterion for its application. This situation is not peculiar to the word 'truth'; in an undecidable calculus, we speak quite unambiguously about 'validity' or 'therorems', although it is logically impossible that we could have criteria for the application of these words. 'To sum up, the theory that in order to determine what a word means we must establish a criterion for its correct use, or for its correct application, is mistaken: we practically never have such a criterion.'[4]

Popper proceeds to define the notion of getting nearer to the truth by developing his 'calculus of verisimilitude', the main idea of which is, in the crudest outline, the following: In the Tarskian sense of 'true', the 'truth-content' of a statement is defined as the class of those true statements which follow deductively from that statement, while the 'falsity-content' of the statement is the class of those false statements which follow from the statement. The 'verisimilitude' of a statement is its truth-content minus its falsity-content. In this sense, if a statement p has a higher verisimilitude than a statement q, then p is nearer to the truth than q. Hence, scientific progress *may* be conceived of as a process of getting nearer to the truth, by replacing theories with low verisimilitude by theories with higher verisimilitude. It is crucial to note, however, that the calculus of verisimilitude does not give us a *measure* of verisimilitude; the concept of 'verisimilitude' is defined with reference to Tarski's concept of 'truth' and, like the latter concept, it lacks a criterion for its application:

> I have in these last sections merely sketched a programme of combining Tarski's theory of truth with his Calculus of Systems so as to obtain a concept of *verisimilitude* which allows us to speak, without fear of talking nonsense, of *theories which are better or worse approximations to truth*. I do not, of course, suggest that there can be a criterion for the applicability of this notion, any more than there is one for the notion of truth.[5]

Science, that is, *may* be regarded as a gradual approximation to truth; it would not be nonsensical to regard science in this way. But to refute relativism one would have to show not only that this notion is meaningful, but also that there are good reasons for believing that science actually does progress in this way. But this would entail giving up the conventionalist definition of scientific progress, since this definition permits a criteriological measure of scientific progress. This measure was developed by Popper in his earlier 'calculus of corroboration', based, essentially, on the notion of the consistency of a theory with the basic statements. Barring the abandonment of conventionalism, the calculus of corroboration would have to be given an interpretation in the calculus of verisimilitude; but this is not possible, since the former calculus involves criteria for progress, while the latter explicitly excludes them. Nor, on the other hand, has Popper been willing to surrender his conventionalism, since this move would re-open the problem of how to reconcile fallibilism with falsificationism – the two central ideas in Popper's philosophy.

How does Popper, in fact, come to terms with this problem? In the first place, by seeking to mitigate his fallibilism, in the second place, by appealing to utterly irrelevant subjectivist notions. Consider:

> But fallibilism need in no way give rise to any sceptical or relativist conclusions. This will become clear if we consider that all the *known* historical examples of human fallibility – including all the *known* examples of miscarriage of justice – are *examples of the advance of our knowledge.* Every discovery of a mistake constitutes a real advance in our knowledge. As Roger Martin du Gard says in *Jean Barois*, 'it is something if we know where truth is not to be found'.[6]

But, according to the consistent fallibilism of *Logik der Forschung, we do not know* where truth is not to be found. On a consistent fallibilism, there are no *known* examples of human fallibility; every statement stating such an example is just as fallible as any other statement. Known examples of human fallibility cannot be cited in support of fallibilism; they constitute a refutation of fallibilism. If we know for certain that we have erred, then there is a rock bottom of knowledge, which is precisely what fallibilism denies.

Consider, secondly,

> And though we may always err, we have in many cases (especially in cases of crucial tests deciding between two theories) a fair idea of whether or not we have in fact got nearer to the truth.[7]

I think this is true, but I also think that we often have a fair idea of whether or not a statement of an observed fact is true. Nonetheless, one of the chief points of *Logik der Forschung* was to show that scientific progress does not depend on subjective certainties, no matter how strong. If Popper is now going to base his belief in the progress of knowledge on such things as 'fair ideas', he would be better off abandoning his earlier conventionalism altogether and saying, instead, that falsifications are based on the truth of observation-statements. We have, after all, a fair idea of the truth of such statements, and if that is the only guarantee we have of scientific progress anyway, we might as well save ourselves all the problems raised by conventionalism.

But Popper has not been willing to go this far, and his 'Tarskian turn' is still far from constituting a refutation of relativism. A fervent anti-relativist and anti-historicist, Popper has not shown how one can accept his philosophy of science without also accepting its relativist and historicist consequences. How, on the other hand, has the new gambit affected his approach to the philosophy of history? The subject is taken up explicitly in Popper's latest book, *Objective Knowledge* (1972).

As Popper sees it, since the Tarskian notion of truth is divorced from criteria, and hence from subjective certainty, it cannot be *beliefs* that are true or false. In speaking of truth, we are speaking of the correspondence between facts and something else, something which does not reside in us, since the correspondence relation may hold without our knowing it. These considerations have led Popper to develop a theory of objective knowledge, of knowledge existing outside us and, in part, independently of us. This theory takes the form of a pluralistic metaphysics of the 'three worlds', or three realms of equally real entities. The first is the physical, or material, world, the second is the subjective, or mental, world. The third world is 'the world of *objective contents of thought,* especially of scientific and poetic thoughts and of works of art'.[8] This third world, Popper admits, bears some resemblance to Plato's world of ideas, or to Hegel's objective spirit. Popper also explicitly compares his third world to that of Gottlob Frege, a comparison which would easily suggest itself anyway, since both the expressions 'third realm' and 'objective thought-content' have gained their contemporary philosophical currency from Frege's writings. Frege introduced his concept of a third realm in order to identify mathematical and logical objects as something distinct from either the physical symbols or the subjective, psychological ideas attending the symbols. The objects inhabiting the third realm he called *Gedanken,* that is, objective thought-contents, closely corresponding

43

to what English-speaking philosophers call 'propositions'. The essence of these thought-contents is that they do not reside in anybody's mind; they can be shared by several thinkers through intersubjective communication, and they can be transmitted from one generation to another through a scientific or artistic or literary tradition.

Knowledge, in this metaphysics, resides in the third world; truth consists in a relation between objects in the third world and objects in the first world. The acquisition and advancement of knowledge consist in the interaction between the second and third worlds: in scientific research, a second-world object (an individual mind) manipulates third-world objects, e.g. by drawing inferences, and the like. The third world is created by the second world, but, once created, the third world lives a life of its own, and generates new objects. This independence is most clearly seen in mathematics: we may have created the natural numbers, but we did not create the odd, even, prime, or irrational numbers. Problem-situations are now something acknowledged as really existing, not something merely representing the researcher's subjective point of view:

> Among the inmates of my 'third world' are, more especially, *theoretical systems;* but inmates just as important are *problems* and *problem situations.* And I will argue that the most important inmates of this world are *critical arguments* and what may be called . . . the *state of a discussion* or the *state of a critical argument* . . .'[9]

For the history of thought, the implication is this: theories, in a sense, arise out of problems, as rational responses to them, while problems arise out of the state of discussion. Explaining the emergence of a particular theory amounts to relating it to a specific problem, and to the state of discussion which gave rise to that problem. But this third-world relation between theories, problems, and states of discussion bears no similarity to causal relations as we find them in the first world. Third-world relations are rational relations, such as presupposition, implication, and the appropriateness or pertinence of answering a particular question in a particular way. History, then, is *sui generis* in the sense that its subject-matter differs from that of the natural sciences; history is concerned with rational beings, having thoughts, posing and solving problems, drawing inferences, and so forth. These thoughts, problems, etc. are members of the third world, and it is their third-world relations that the historian is interested in establishing, by the rational reconstruction of problem-situations or states of discussion: 'My thesis is that the main aim of all historical understanding is the hypothetical reconstruction of a historical *problem-situation*.'[10]

Popper illustrates this method by the historical example of Galileo's theory of the tides. I do not think it is coincidental that he chooses an example from the history of thought; rather, it seems to be part of Popper's view that the history of thought is paradigmatic for history in general. Briefly, Galileo held that the tides were caused by periodical accelerations and retardations in the rotational velocity of the earth. The problem of historical explanation is: Why did Galileo advance such an odd theory, instead of accepting what everybody had believed all along, and that Kepler's laws had just confirmed, namely that the tides are due to the influence of the moon? The usual psychological interpretation in terms of Galileo's vanity, or dogmatism, or jealousy towards Kepler, is irrelevant in Popper's view; the explanation is to be found elsewhere: 'I claim that the first and all-important step is to ask ourselves: *what was the (third-world) problem* to which Galileo's theory was a tentative solution? And what was the situation – the logical *problem situation* – in which this problem arose?'[11] Popper then proceeds to explain Galileo's theory as a perfectly justified attempt at exploiting to the full the explanatory potential of a few simple ideas, namely Copernican astronomy and his own two laws of the conservation of motion. Furthermore, in a situation where the forerunners of modern enlightenment were combating medieval obscurantism, it was perfectly rational to stick to the principle of simplicity of explanation, rather than to invoke the mystical forces attributed to the moon by astrologers. By so understanding the rationality of Galileo's dogmatism, we have explained it historically:

Thus we are led by the analysis of Galileo's problem situation to justify the rationality of Galileo's method in several points in which he has been criticized by various historians; and thus we are led to a better *historical understanding* of Galileo. Psychological explanations which have been attempted, such as ambition, jealousy, or aggressiveness, or the wish to create a stir, become superfluous. They are here replaced by a third-world situational analysis.[12]

So far, so good. Although I am not qualified to endorse or debate this particular explanation of Galileo, I agree that this is the *kind* of explanation which one should aim at. But the same kind of explanation would be arrived at by exploiting the positive heuristic of Popper's earlier works. The question now is: What is new here? What is gained by placing the method of situational analysis within the metaphysical framework of the three worlds? How, in particular, does Popper make sense of the analysis within this new framework?

Popper begins by claiming that his reconstruction of Galileo's problem-situation (P_1) is a conjecture, and this seems fair enough. Then he goes on:

> But if my reconstruction of P_1 is a conjecture, *what is the problem which this conjecture tries to solve?* Obviously, it is P^u, the *problem of understanding* Galileo's theory. My *third* point is this: *our problem of understanding*, P^u, is *on a higher level* than P_1. That is to say, the problem of understanding is a *metaproblem*.[13]

And again, a little further on:

> 'My *fourth* point is that every attempt (except the most trivial one) to understand a theory is bound to open up a historical investigation about this theory and its problem, which thus become part of the *object* of the investigation. ... The problems which these historical investigations try to solve will be metaproblems, to be sharply distinguished from the problems which are the objects under investigation.[14]

In other words, the historian need not even try to solve Galileo's problem about the tides; the historian's problem is the metaproblem: What was Galileo's theory of the tides? This historical problem belongs on a different level of thought from Galileo's problem, and solving the historical problem need not involve solving Galileo's problem.

My central conclusion in this section is this: while Popper now recognizes the *sui generis* nature of the *subject-matter* of historical research, the introduction of third-world levels of thought permits him to reintroduce an essential *unity of method* between the natural and the human sciences. And the method is the hypothetico-deductive method, half-heartedly and unconvincingly defended in *The Poverty of Historicism*. This method, which Popper now usually calls the method of conjecture and refutation, is schematized as follows:

$$P_1 \to TT \to EE \to P_2,$$

where we proceed from an intial problem, P_1, to a conjectural solution, or tentative theory, TT, to a refutation, or error-elimination, EE, to a novel problem, P_2. We have already seen, in Chapter 1, how this schema is realized in the natural sciences; now the contention is that essentially the same method is applied in historical investigation. We have an initial problem about a third-world object, say, Galileo's theory of the tides; we try to solve it by proposing a tentative theory about the relation of Galileo's theory to other third-world objects, the problem-situation; we criticize or refute our tentative (meta) theory by comparing it with documentary evidence (on the curious but necessary assumption that documents belong to the third world); and, in case of a clash between the documents and our theory, we shall emerge with a new problem to be tackled in the same manner.

It is essential to this view of historical method that the third world can be sharply differentiated into object levels and meta-levels, so that the theory at the meta-level can admit of falsification by negative feedback from the object level. Without such feedback, the tentative theory could not be criticized (except internally, on the ground of possible inconsistency), and the research could not proceed beyond the first theory formation. I do not think such a stratification of the third world is possible, and I shall presently offer some arguments to this effect. At the moment, I wish to argue that Popper gets around the difficulty by maintaining a certain vagueness as to the exact ontological status of third-world objects.

In intially characterizing the objects of the third world, Popper enumerates 'problems, conjectures, theories, arguments, *journals*, and *books*' (my italics).[15] Now journals and books – in general, documents – may be regarded either as physical objects, belonging to the first world, or as carriers of meaning-contents, belonging to the third world. Since Popper has explicitly compared his third world to Frege's world of thoughts, it may seem fair to interpret him as referring to books and journals in the second sense, as bearers of meaning. However, Popper presented this list with the express intention of showing the uncontroversial nature of the third world. The physical existence of journals and books is hardly controversial, but the ontological status of their meaning-contents is one of the most hotly debated questions in recent philosophy. Are they sentences, statements, judgments, or propositions? Popper does not address himself to this question. Furthermore, it is only as first-world objects that documents constitute an ontological level distinct from theories about them, and it is only in this respect that they can provide a neutral testing-ground for theories, as required by the hypothetico-deductive model. On the other hand, it is only the *interpreted contents* of documents which can be regarded as belonging to the third world and partaking of logical relations to problems, etc. This realization undercuts the attempt at giving a hypothetico-deductive account of interpretation, since the hypothetico-deductive account is now seen to *presuppose* an interpretation of the documents.

Now the retort might possibly be made: 'Well, what is wrong with presupposing a *rudimentary* level of textual interpretation and reconstructing the subsequent steps of the analysis in terms of the hypothetico-deductive schema? After all, a methodology gives, at best, an idealized model of the method, and it cannot be expected to incorporate everything.' To this possible retort I have two rejoinders.

In the first place, if we grant the legitimacy of presupposing, on a rudimentary level, the accessibility of the contents of documents, the subsequent steps may indeed be conceived of as a process of 'conjectures and refutations', where approximative hypotheses are imaginatively invented, tried out on the text, rejected, and replaced by better approximations. This observation is not even entirely trivial: I have no wish to deny the heuristic fruitfulness of a certain self-consciousness as to the role of preconceived, tentative hypotheses. But the structural similarity of this trial-and-error process to the hypothetico-deductive method in natural science is, as far as I can see, superficial. The structural dissimilarities seem to me far more significant. For instance, in natural science (as Popper agrees) one proceeds from hypotheses of relatively low generality to hypotheses of ever higher generality. Hypotheses about 'all ravens' are of little interest to science, hypotheses about 'all birds' are somewhat more interesting, and when we start hypothesizing about 'all vertebrates', we are really moving on the level of scientific theory formation. On the lower levels, when we encounter a refutation, we do not propose another, less general, hypothesis; this would be an '*ad hoc* stratagem'; instead, we move on to a higher level of generality, and this is what Popper recognizes as progress. In history, the situation is the opposite. Faced with the problem of how to explain Stalin's terror (to which we shall return), we are not saying anything very interesting by citing the very general 'Acton's Law': 'Power corrupts, and absolute power corrupts absolutely.' This may be all right as a first approximation, but in the further process of research, we seek to replace it by hypotheses of ever decreasing generality. We do not think we have any good explanation of Stalin's terror until we have arrived at an hypothesis which, at the very least, fails to explain Tsar Ivan's terror or the French terror. In this sense, historical explanations are essentially ad hoc. The higher the generality of the explanatory hypothesis, the less understanding do we have of the individual historical event. So the criteria for selecting and eliminating hypotheses in historical research are radically unlike the criteria embodied in the hypothetico-deductive model of natural science.

In the second place, I have profound qualms about the legitimacy of simply presupposing the accessibility of the contents of documents. These qualms do not stem from any general skepticism toward the possibility of textual interpretation, but rather from the belief that, by assuming any level of textual interpretation to be unproblematic, we run the danger of concealing the theoretically most interesting features of historical method. This can best be elucidated by an example. In a document, I run across the sentence Καί θεός ἦν ὁ λόγος. One might think that the interpretation of this sentence is a trivial affair; I only have to know Greek, and I know that the sentence means 'And the Word was God'. The trouble is, we're still stuck with merely a sentence – i.e. a string of physical signs, belonging to the first world – not a meaningful content, belonging to the third world. In order to get at the content, we have to know, at least, whether the 'is' is the 'is' of identity, or the 'is' of attribution, i.e. whether the meaning is that the Word was one with God, or that the Word was God-like. The ambiguity is in the original Greek; if it had said ὁ θεός or else θεῖος, the matter would be clear. What makes this ambiguity theoretically interesting is the fact that the former interpretation supports the orthodox theological belief in the Trinity, while the latter interpretation supports the liberal belief that Jesus was an excellent human being, who, through his moral excellence, exhibited the God-like qualities of man and, to that extent, partook of God's nature. And I see no possibility of an orthodox and a liberal agreeing on one and the same interpretation, *while remaining,* respectively, orthodox and liberal. Furthermore, the difference between the two theologies *also* involves a difference in one's approach to biblical interpretation.

The reader may be suspicious of the historical scrupulousness of theologians, but the logical relation involved is not affected by such suspicions. The two theologians may indeed agree on one interpretation, but one of them will, in that process, have to revise his theological beliefs and hence his approach to textual interpretation. My point is not that human weakness may tempt one to misinterpret historical evidence in order to justify one's present beliefs; the point is to note the logical relation which permits such temptations to arise. This relation may be put the other way around. Important historical documents are frequently not *just* historical evidence; at the same time, they are elements in an intellectual tradition in terms of which our present beliefs and convictions are formulated. A reinterpretation of the evidence frequently alters our present vantage point and, hence, effects a revision of our approach to historical interpretation itself. Hence the question, 'What does the document say?' is not, in all cases, separable from the question, 'Is what it says true?'. So the distinction between the theoretical and factual levels, crucial to the hypothetico-deductive method, breaks down when applied to documentary interpretation.

The example from the Bible is particularly clear-cut, but the same situation can be observed with all documents which occupy an important place in our intellectual tradition (and, of course, we have no mechanical criterion for deciding which documents do occupy an important place, and which don't). Present-day intellectuals might feel more comfortable with the following example. Confront a Marxian democratic socialist historian with Marx's obscure passages on the 'dictatorship of the proletariat', and offer him this interpretation: a) The dictatorship of the proletariat is logically entailed by Marx's theory of the class struggle, as a necessary consequence, not merely as a possible contingency; b) Lenin's one-party dictatorship on behalf of the proletariat is the concrete embodiment of the dictatorship of the proletariat. Most likely he will reject this interpretation. But suppose he accepts it? He is then faced with the choice of either abandoning his belief in democracy, like Mao or Marcuse, or abandoning Marxian socialism, like Djilas. And this decision also concerns the question of whether or not to interpret history in terms of the class struggle. Of course, the moral is not simply that one must be consistent in one's beliefs; the moral is that present-day beliefs and convictions are formulated in concepts which presuppose an intellectual tradition; a reinterpretation of this tradition frequently necessitates a revision of one's present-day beliefs and convictions, including those brought to bear on historical interpretation.

In short, the interpretation of historical documents interferes with the conceptual apparatus which we ourselves bring to the task of interpretation. We cannot, therefore, treat the documents as a level of 'facts', distinct from, and in mutual independence of, our theories about these 'facts'. The world of intellectual products, or 'third-world objects', cannot be stratified into theoretical and factual levels, as is required by the negative feedback mechanism of the hypothetico-deductive method. Eliminating the problem of textual interpretation by a methodological presumption would only mean abdicating one's pretensions to elucidate the historical method.

To sum up this chapter. Popper's 'Tarskian turn' leaves unresolved the problem of relativism inherent in his earlier views. His 'Fregean turn' brings him full circle back to his original deductivist approach to historical explanation, and the new version is hardly more convincing than the original one. The introduction of the metaphysics of the three worlds shows, by the way, that the driving force in Popper's philosophy is not (as some claim) 'positivism', in the sense of anti-metaphysics, but rather his belief in the unity of knowledge, and more specifically, the unity of method. Since my discussion of Popper has so far been largely critical, I wish to repeat that this is not due to any wish to belittle a man whom I regard as one of the greatest thinkers of the age. Rather, the weaknesses of Popper's philosophy bear witness to the magnitude and complexity of the problems which he has had the intellectual courage to tackle with greater ambition – and with deeper penetration – than most. The very importance of these problems constitutes a reason for examining in what ways the best attempts at solving them have so far failed. This will, in all modesty, be attempted in the following two chapters.

5. Popper's Dispute with Collingwood

As has been pointed out both by Popper himself[1] and, earlier, by Joseph Agassi,[2] there is a considerable resemblance between Popper's 'situational analysis' and Collingwood's proposed method of the 're-enactment of past thought'. There is no reference to Collingwood in any of Popper's earlier works; in *Objective Knowledge,* however, he makes a special effort to dissociate his own views from Collingwood. The argument is illuminating in that it exhibits what I regard as the most serious flaws in Popper's position.

Initially, Popper states his disagreement with Collingwood as follows:

> ... it is generally believed that we cannot do without such sub-jective procedures as *sympathetic understanding* or empathy, or the re-enactment of other people's actions (Collingwood), or the attempt to put ourselves into another person's situation by making his aims and his problems our own. As against this view my thesis is this. Exactly as a subjective state of understanding finally reached, so a psychological process which leads up to it must be analysed in terms of the third-world objects in which it is anchored. In fact it can be analysed *only* in these terms.[3]

As I intend to show in detail, this is precisely Collingwood's view as well. Throughout his life, Collingwood vigorously opposed psychologism, i.e. the attempt to study the mind without attending to the truth or falsity of the contents of thought. In his earliest book, *Religion and Philosophy,* he criticizes William James in this respect, concluding, 'the mind, regarded in this way, ceases to be a mind at all'.[4] In one of his later books, *An Essay on Metaphysics,* the same line of attack is continued: 'Psychology cannot be a science of thought, because the methods it has developed in its history as a science of feeling preclude it from dealing with the problems of criteriology. It has nothing to say about truth and falsehood.'[5] In the light of these passages it seems odd, to say the least, that Popper, in rejecting psychologism, should believe that he was opposing Collingwood.

Consider Popper's further elucidation of the issue. After granting a considerable degree of agreement with Collingwood, he then goes on:

> We part company over the issue of second and third worlds: the issue of choosing a subjective or objective method. (We agree on the significance of problem situations.) Collingwood's psychological way of putting things is by no means a matter of mere formulation. Rather, it is an essential part of his theory of understanding.[6]

And again,

> Collingwood makes it clear that the essential thing in understanding history is not the analysis of the situation itself, but the historian's mental process of re-enactment, the sympathetic repetition of the original experience. For Collingwood, the analysis of the situation serves merely as a help – an indispensable help – for this re-enactment. My view is diametrically opposed.[7]

Now Collingwood does, in *The Idea of History,* employ a mentalistic vocabulary, and he speaks of the re-enactment of other people's acts of thought as essential to the historical understanding. But this terminology presupposes a monistic philosophy, and it makes no sense to interpret it within Popper's pluralism, or within the common-sense dualism which most of us unreflectively presuppose. When Collingwood speaks of acts of thought, he presupposes a one-to-one correspondence between these acts and the contents of thought. The mentalistic terminology is not introduced for the purpose of discussing history in psychological terms, but for the exactly opposite purpose of discussing mind nonpsychologically, in terms of the truth or falsity of thought-contents. I believe that Collingwood is mistaken in presupposing the one-to-one correspondence between acts and contents of thought, and I believe that this mistake somewhat vitiates the presentation in *The Idea of History.* But I believe, also, that what is essential in Collingwood's theory of the historical understanding can be expressed in terms of thought-contents alone, as Collingwood himself presents it in his theory of presuppositions. In spite of what Popper says, however, there is no second-world versus third-world issue between him and Collingwood; the latter's 'acts of thought' are not second-world objects in Popper's sense; they are at least as much third-world objects. The disagreement is not over the choice of a second-world or third-world method, but over the possibility of a stratification of the third world into object levels and meta-levels; Popper believes in the possibility of such stratification; Collingwood, as we shall see, does not.

My assertion that Popper has misinterpreted and misconstrued Collingwood by taking his statements about re-enactment out of their intended context will have to await corroboration until the chapters dealing specifically with Collingwood. At this point, I wish to argue that Popper's misunderstanding of Collingwood is not purely accidental: it proceeds from the failure, in Popper's own philosophy, to distinguish two quite different problems, on the one hand, the problem of distinguishing between second-world thought-processes and third-world thought-contents, and on the other, the problem of distinguishing between the different levels of third-world objects. Put briefly, Popper employs perfectly good arguments in favor of the first distinction in order to uphold the highly dubious second distinction, on which his hypothetico-deductive approach rests. What Popper needs to establish is the distinction between the level of problems facing the agent (the object level) and the level of problems facing the historian (the meta-level). To uphold this distinction, no problem on the object level may appear on the meta-level. Popper begins by pointing out the danger (a real one from his point of view) of confusing the two levels. 'It is only too easy to mix these two up, for if we formulate the historian's problem by asking: "What was Galileo's problem?", the answer seems to be 'P$_1$'; but P$_1$ (as opposed to "Galileo's problem was P$_1$") seems to belong on the object level rather than the meta-level; and so the two get confused'.[8] Popper then advances his main contention: *'But there are, in general, no problems common to the two different levels.'*[9] Is this true? Popper tries to support it by the trivial observation that the meta-level is essentially richer than the object level, and so contains problems not appearing on the latter level. This is trivial because that is how we define 'meta-level'. But from the observation that the meta-theory may contain structural units not to be found in the theory to be interpreted, it does not follow that the converse is the case; nor does it seem that the converse could possibly be the case. For the meta-theory to be essentially richer than the object theory, it must at least contain within it the latter. To take Popper's example: Galileo's problem may be formulated: 'What causes the tides?', and the historian's problem may be formulated: 'What was Galileo's problem?' But, in the latter formulation, the phrase 'Galileo's problem' is simply shorthand for 'What causes the tides?', and posing the question 'What was Galileo's problem?' involves, a fortiori, posing the question 'What causes the tides?'. The rational reconstruction of Galileo's problem, i.e. the search for the presuppositions on which Galileo's answer was a rational one, necessarily involves a serious attempt at solving Galileo's problem. This is essentially Collingwood's position; evidently, it can be stated without any reference to the repetition of psychological processes.

This is the issue which Popper confounds by invoking the innocuous distinction between thought-processes and thought-contents:

> ... even if we could speak at all sensibly (which I am inclined to deny) of such a thing as a *similarity* between third-world *thought-contents* on the one hand and, on the other, those second-world *thought-processes* through which we grasp these contents, even then I should still deny that there actually is, in general, any similarity, on any level of problems, between the contents and the corresponding thought-processes.[10]

This claim, of course, is quite easy to defend, and this is the claim which Popper actually defends against his strawman version of Collingwood, instead of defending his theory against Collingwood's far more serious attack on the stratification of the third world.

The thesis of the stratification of the third world is essential to Popper's thesis of the unity of method. Collingwood, as will be shown, is the most formidable modern critic of that stratification; yet, in his critical discussion of Collingwood, Popper makes no attempt at defending this thesis. Why not? I have alrady hinted that the thesis cannot be defended; this claim will be argued by a more detailed examination of the third world.

6. Inventory of the Third World

As I mentioned in the last chapter but one, there is a problem as to what things are or are not inmates of the third world. In the words of Anthony Quinton: 'the qualifications for admission to world 3 are radically unclear. The things he puts in it are in some cases Platonic, that is things that could possibly be thought even if no one ever does think them, and in others Hegelian, things that someone has thought and expressed.'[1] The latter objects, Quinton also suggests, seem in no way to differ from the inmates of the first world. The reason for this vagueness, I have suggested, is that, while Popper needs something like a Fregean third world in order to support his epistemology of disembodied knowledge, at the same time he needs to be able unambiguously to identify *some* third-world objects, in order to contrast them with others – otherwise, he would not get the (for his purposes) all-important stratification of the third world into object levels and meta-levels. In this chapter I shall try to show that Frege's third world admits of no such stratification.

This argument requires a brief introduction to Frege's semantics of 'sense' and 'reference', as presented in his classic paper 'Ueber Sinn und Bedeutung'. Words and sentences, according to Frege, both express a sense and designate a reference; a word expresses a concept and designates an object; a sentence expresses a thought, or proposition, and designates a truth-value, viz. either the True or the False. 'It is natural, now, to think of there being connected with a sign (name, combination of words, letter), besides that to which the sign refers, which may be called the reference of the sign, also what I should call the *sense* of the sign, wherein the mode of presentation is contained.'[2] The sense of a sentence, i.e. its thought, is to be sharply distinguished from the subjective, psychological process of thinking that thought: 'By a thought I understand not the subjective performance of thinking but its objective content, which is capable of being the common property of several thinkers.'[3] The thought, therefore, has to be distinguished both from that which is thought of, i.e. the reference, and from the subjective ideas attending the thought in any one individual mind.

For Frege, the latter distinction is unproblematic, as it seems obviously to be achieved by the publicness of thoughts, as opposed to the privacy of ideas (in the sense of the associations of a thought): 'For one can hardly deny that mankind has a common store of thoughts which is transmitted from one generation to another.'[4] It is the distinction between a thought and its reference that is problematic. However, for a sentence to express a thought, i.e. have a sense, it is sufficient that its component parts have a sense, and no reference is strictly required. So, for instance, 'Odysseus was set ashore at Ithaca while sound asleep' is plainly meaningful, and hence expresses a thought, even though it is not normally presumed that the word 'Odysseus' refers to anything. Thus, though it has a sense, it does not have a reference; that is to say, although we understand it as a significant sentence, we would not raise the question of its truth or falsity. Anyone who did raise that question would have to presuppose not only the meaningfulness of the name 'Odysseus', but also the existence of the person so designated. In general, the instantiation of its referring expressions is a precondition for the truth or falsity of any thought or proposition; whenever we take a proposition seriously as a candidate for truth or falsity, we always presuppose that its referring expressions have a reference:

> If anything is asserted there is always an obvious presupposition that the simple and compound proper names used have reference. If one therefore asserts 'Kepler died in misery', there is a presupposition that the name 'Kepler' designates something; but it does not follow that the sense of the sentence 'Kepler died in misery' contains the thought that the name 'Kepler' designates something.[5]

The point here is that, if the existence of Kepler were part of what is asserted, rather than a presupposition of the assertion, it would follow counter-intuitively that the denial of 'Kepler died in misery' would have to run not 'Kepler did not die in misery', but 'Kepler did not die in misery, or the name Kepler has no reference'.[6] But, in fact, whenever we take such a sentence up for assertion or denial, we always understand the existence of the person referred to to be presupposed by the denial as much as by the assertion.

The two points made so far are: the possibility of a sentence having a sense without having a reference secures the ontological distinctness of the two; *but* we do not normally assert a sentence without presupposing not only a sense, but a reference as well. Indeed, Frege holds that the possibility of a symbol lacking a reference is an imperfection of natural languages; in a symbolic, 'perfect' language, this situation ought not to occur.

Bertrand Russell (who has in fact rejected Frege's analysis of presuppositions, and accepted the counter-intuitive interpretation of negations) has advanced a powerful argument against the tenability of the sense–reference distinction. Russell's argument can hardly be stated with greater compactness and clarity than that with which he himself presents it; it will, therefore, be reproduced verbatim, noting that Russell uses the terms 'meaning' and 'denotation' for what have here been called 'sense' and 'reference'.

When we wish to speak about the *meaning* of a denoting phrase, as opposed to its *denotation,* the natural mode of doing so is by inverted commas. ... We say, to begin with, that when C occurs it is the *denotation* that we are speaking about; but when 'C' occurs, it is the *meaning.* Now the relation of meaning and denotation is not merely linguistic through the phrase: there must be a logical relation involved, which we express by saying that the meaning denotes the denotation. But the difficulty which confronts us is that we cannot succeed in *both* preserving the connexion of meaning and denotation *and* prevent them from being one and the same; also that the meaning cannot be got at except by means of denoting phrases. This happens as follows.

The one phrase C was to have both meaning and denotation. But if we speak of 'the meaning of C', that gives us the meaning (if any) of the denotation. 'The meaning of the first line of Gray's Elegy' is the same as 'The meaning of "The curfew tolls the knell of parting day",' and is not the same as 'The meaning of "the first line of Gray's Elegy".' Thus in order to get the meaning we want, we must speak not of 'the meaning of C', but of 'the meaning of "C",' which is the same as 'C' by itself. Similarly, 'the denotation of C' does not mean the denotation we want, but means something which, if it denotes at all, denotes what is denoted by the denotation we want. For example, let 'C' be 'the denoting complex occurring in the second of the above instances'. Then

C = 'the first line of Gray's Elegy', and

the denotation of C = The curfew tolls the knell of parting day. But what we *meant* to have as the denotation was 'the first line of Gray's Elegy'. Thus we have failed to get what we wanted.[7]

Russell concludes categorically: 'This is an inextricable tangle, and seems to prove that the whole distinction of meaning and denotation has been wrongly conceived.'[8] This, I think, is rashly stated; from the fact that we have no criterion for the application of the sense–reference distinction to particular instances, it does not follow that such a distinction cannot, in general, be upheld. The same, after all, holds of concepts like 'truth', 'validity', 'consistency', etc. However, this possible rejoinder to Russell is too easy; by seemingly refuting his sweeping conclusion, it fails to come to terms with the slightly more modest, and more serious, conclusion actually entailed by Russell's argument. The conclusion is this: in one particular domain, we not only lack a general criterion for applying the sense–reference distinction, but, within this domain, there is no one particular instance to which the distinction can be applied. The domain is that of thoughts referring to thoughts, and the impossibility, in this domain, of upholding the distinctness between sense and reference effectively prohibits any stratification of the realm of thoughts into anything like object levels and meta-levels.

To vary Russell's example with Popper's. The meta-level is supposed to contain not merely linguistic signs, but also the senses of those signs, i.e. the third-world thoughts expressed by the signs. So the linguistic *phrase* 'Galileo's problem' is to have both a sense and a reference; it is supposed to express one thought and refer to a different thought. Now, on the one hand, 'the sense of Galileo's problem' is the same as 'the sense of "What causes the tides?",' and is not the same as 'the sense of "Galileo's problem".' On the other hand, 'the sense of "Galileo's problem" ' is the same as simply 'Galileo's problem', which refers to, and hence picks out, the thought 'What causes the tides?'. (It will not help us to introduce the use—mention distinction, since we are here trying to talk about senses, not expressions.)

Hence, any attempt at identifying the thought on the meta-level causes it to coalesce with the thought on the object level. Hence, also, the Tarskian definition of truth, which presupposes such a distinctness of levels, can apply only to sentences, not to Fregean thoughts.

In consequence, to the extent that a work of history is, in Frege's sense, a body of thoughts about thoughts, there is no effective method of identifying the thoughts constituting the historical investigation apart from the thoughts that form the object of investigation. This, of course, is precisely the conclusion which was argued on methodological grounds in Chapter 4.

However, in his later paper 'The Thought: A Logical Inquiry', Frege makes a fresh attempt at identifying thoughts. The approach now is extensional; that is, Frege tries to identify thoughts via their references, or truth-values. The success of such a program would tend to draw the teeth of Russell's criticism. I shall argue, however, that the attempt is not successful.

This is the paper in which Frege introduces the expression 'third realm', foreshadowing Popper's 'third world':

> A third realm must be recognized. What belongs to this corresponds with ideas in that it cannot be perceived by the senses, but with things in that it needs no bearer to the contents of whose consciousness it belongs. Thus the thought, for example, which we expressed in the Pythagorean theorem is timelessly true, true independently of whether anyone takes it to be true. It needs no bearer.[9]

So the autonomy of the third realm is secured by the timeless truth-or-falsity of thoughts, a truth-or-falsity which is not dependent on anyone's cognition. This constitutes the distinguishing characteristic of a thought: 'Without wishing to give a definition, I call a thought something for which the question of truth arises.'[10] This constitutes a departure from the earlier paper, where it was held that a sentence may have a sense and yet no truth-value, as, for instance, 'Odysseus was set ashore at Ithaca while sound asleep'. This situation was, however, even then described as an anomaly, something which should not, and need not, occur. In his later paper, Frege does not seem to take even the possibility of such anomalies seriously. The identification of thoughts via truth-values is explained by this example:

With the sentence 'Alfred has still not come' one really says 'Alfred has not come' and, at the same time, hints that his arrival is expected, but it is only hinted. It cannot be said that, since Alfred's arrival is not expected, the sense of the sentence is therefore false. The word 'but' differs from 'and' in that in it one intimates that what follows is in contrast with what would be expected from what preceded it. Such suggestions in speech make no difference to the thought.[11]

Or, even clearer, 'they do not touch the thought, *they do not touch what is true or false.*'[12] (My italics).

From these quotes, we seem to be led to the following principle of individuation: two sentences express one and the same thought if and only if they have the same truth-values; if, that is, it is impossible for one to be true and the other to be false. Such an extensionalist principle would circumvent the problem indicated by Russell, since it would, on this principle, be possible to paraphrase all our talk about thoughts into talk about sentences and truth-values. It would also render the notion of 'thought', or, in general, of 'sense', quite redundant.

But Frege finds himself unable to defend this extensionalist principle against certain recalcitrant examples. Suppose Dr. Gustav Lauben says, 'I have been wounded'. Leo Peters hears this and remarks some days later, 'Dr. Gustav Lauben has been wounded'. Now suppose Rudolph Lingens was present on both occasions and heard both utterances, but does not know Dr. Gustav Lauben by name. He cannot then know that the same person has been referred to on both occasions, and he may well believe the one sentence to be true and the other false. For this reason, because their *supposed* truth-values may differ, Frege concludes that the two sentences express different thoughts: 'I say, therefore, in this case: the thought which Leo Peters expresses is not the same as that which Dr. Lauben uttered.'[13] Similarly, suppose that Herbert Garner knows Lauben by name and birthplace, but does not know his title or his present whereabouts. It is then quite possible for Garner to take the sentence 'Dr. Lauben has been wounded' to be true, while taking the sentence 'Gustav Lauben has been wounded' to be false. Again, according to Frege: 'Under the assumptions given these thoughts are therefore different.'[14]

What are the assumptions given? The chief assumption is that the thought, which may be common to several sentences, must be *time-lessly* true or false, so that expressions like 'here', 'today', 'I', or proper names – what are sometimes called 'egocentric particulars' – must be supplemented with factual information to secure unambiguous reference.[15] But the implications of this are devastating for the extensionalist approach as outlined a couple of pages back. For now it becomes apparent that the individuation of thoughts depends not on truth-values alone, but on whether or not any given subject possesses the background knowledge required to identify the truth-value. In other words, the thought is affected by the mere possibility of some one subject's not possessing that background knowledge. This admission entails an entirely different principle of individuation from the one suggested earlier; it entails the following, intensionalist principle: Two sentences express one and the same thought if and only if it is impossible for one and the same person without contradiction to hold the one to be true and the other false. Some such formulation as this seems to be necessitated by the Gustav Lauben example, but this formulation runs counter to the extensionalist approach which Frege adopted at the outset of the paper, and which he would have to make good in order to avoid Russell's criticism. According to my second formulation, thoughts are not identified via sentences and truth-values; *thoughts are identified only via thoughts*. This, I think, is not only a necessary consequence of Frege's argument; it is also, I believe, true. This conclusion further supports Russell's argument, with my qualifications; and it further explains why Popper got into a muddle over both the inventory of the third world and the interpretation of Collingwood. Both muddles stem from a vain attempt at doing something impossible, namely, identifying a level of thought that is independent of our thought of it.

7. Collingwood's Philosophy of Mind

R. G. Collingwood's philosophy is known to the public chiefly from his unfinished, posthumously published *The Idea of History* (1946). Despite – or perhaps because of – the deceptive lucidity of its style, this work is far from easy to understand; specifically, I do not think it can be properly assessed except in the context of Collingwood's thought as a whole. I propose, therefore, to approach this work from the twin vantage points of the philosophy of mind presented in Collingwood's earlier writings, and the theory of presuppositions contained in his later writings. This approach carries the underlying assumption of an essential continuity in Collingwood's thought; this assumption will not here be made the subject of explicit argument, although it will receive incidental corroboration. (Those interested in an explicit argument are referred to the works of Louis Mink[1] and Lionel Rubinoff.[2]) Some specific changes in his thought will, however, be noted.

In Collingwood's earliest book, *Religion and Philosophy* (1916), the chief purpose is to refute the psychologistic approach to religion, as exemplified especially by William James. James and other psychologists of the day attempted (like Erikson and Fromm today) to study religion as merely a class of subjective states of mind, without raising the question of the truth or falsity of religious creeds, without, that is, taking seriously the intellectual content of religion. In repudiating psychologism, Collingwood adopted a position of radical monism, following, to some extent, Aristotle and anticipating, to a lesser extent, Ryle. What Collingwood attempted to show was that the religious mind cannot be studied in abstraction from its content – the specific creed – because the mind and its object are identical and a fortiori indistinguishable. We shall consider the argument from the point of view of its general philosophical interest.

'Thought' and 'Will', according to this argument, are not the names of mental entities, but are predicative expressions, which qualify actions. Thinking and willing are not things we do with our thought and will, in the sense that we walk with our legs. We always think or will something definite, and we cannot conceive of thinking and willing pure and simple, without referring them to some object. What we will is always some action, say, walking. Willing and walking are not then two different operations, one mental and one physical; they are one and the same, namely, the activity of walking freely performed. Thinking is not, in its turn, something over and above this action; in thinking, we are conscious of what we will and, *eo ipso*, of what we do; the consciousness of walking is no different from the action of walking consciously performed. Thought and will, in short, consist merely in the free and conscious execution of actions. In this sense, 'the mind *is* what it *does*';[3] not in the sense that there are specifically mental actions, but in the sense that all actions involve presence of mind in so far as they are freely and consciously performed – 'freely' and 'consciously' to be taken, presumably, in their common-sense meaning.

When I am conscious of walking, one might say that walking is the object of my consciousness, but this is not to imply that there are here two distinct entities, consciousness as a subject and walking as an object. There is only the conscious activity of walking. The same relation holds, according to Collingwood, for all cases where we ordinarily speak of a 'subject' and an 'object': there is really only the conscious activity, which is differently referred to as the consciousness of an object, or as the object of consciousness. The dichotomy between thinking pure and simple, and an object which may or may not be thought of, is obliterated: thinking is always the thinking of a definite object, and an object is always an object of thought. 'All consciousness is the consciousness of something definite, the thought of this thing or of that thing; there is no thought in general, but only particular thoughts about particular things. The *esse* of the mind is not *cogitare* simply, but *de hac re cogitare*.'[4] The object of thought is not an 'idea', in the sense of an image or likeness of the thing; the object of thought *is* the thing in so far as it is thought of: 'My thought of the table is certainly not something "like" the table; it is the table as I know it.'[5]

At this stage of the exposition, some critical questions may be raised:

1. If the mind is identical with its object, must not all objects of thought – hence all objects – be private? On the identity-view, how can different persons, having different minds, know the same objects?

2. Even if it were possible for different minds to know the same objects, how, on the identity-view, is it possible for different minds to know the same object differently, or, as we say, to place different constructions on the same facts?

3. If the mind is identical with its object, what, if anything, is the object with which the mind is identical, when in error? How does Collingwood tackle these questions?

1. It is not possible for different minds to know the same object. When two minds attend to the same object, then, to just that extent and in just that respect, those two minds are identical; more precisely, the hypothesis is false: there are, in this case, not two minds, only one. Furthermore, taking the individuality of the mind as the principle for the individuation of persons, it follows that one and the same object of thought can have as its subject only one person. If you and I attend to the same object, to that extent and in that respect, we are not two persons, but only one. To complete our quotation on the previous page:

> Similarly, your thought of the table is what you know of the table, the table as known to you; and if we both have real knowledge of the table, it seems to follow that our thoughts are the same, not merely similar; and further, if the mind is its thoughts, we seem to have, for this moment at least, actually one mind; we share between us that unity of consciousness which we said to be the mark of the individual.[6]

This thesis of the interpersonal identity of knowing subjects may seem an extravagant flourish, unworthy of serious attention. For my own part, however, I take this to be the most significant thesis of the book. For the purposes of the present discussion, its cash value is that thoughts, as well as their objects, are essentially public. The life of the mind belongs to the public sphere; there is no privileged access and no right of privacy to protect against intrusion. Collingwood's monism (like Ryle's, though perhaps even more radically) cuts across the Gordian knot of Cartesian dualism and the consequent problem of 'other minds': there just aren't any other minds, in the relevant respects. Put more concretely, and more to the point, any intellectual product, such as a poem, a philosophical argument, or a scientific theory, is publicly graspable and is, in principle, the property of anyone who makes the effort to understand it. If there is to be any special point to this theory, we must take it, I think (as indeed other evidence seems to justify), that what is public is the purely intellectual content of thoughts, abstracted from all accompanying ideas and emotions. So understood, Collingwood contrasts with Wilhelm Dilthey, who held that in order to understand the thoughts of another person, one must achieve an empathetic, emotional identification with the other. Collingwood's contrary claim is that the understanding has no need to be mediated by such a subjective identification; on the contrary, the subjective identification follows as a consequence of the understanding, which, in its turn, is objectively mediated by the public, hence 'objective', thought-content shared by the two subjects.

2. To the extent that two persons know the same object, to precisely that extent do they know it in the same manner. The common distinction between 'fact' and 'construction' is erroneous: Two persons placing different 'constructions' on 'the same facts' do not, properly speaking, know the same facts. Suppose A believes in the theory of human selfishness, and B believes in altruism; and suppose C performs an action which is construed by A as an instance of selfishness, and by B as an instance of altruism, whereby they are both strengthened in their respective beliefs. Does this show that moral theories are impervious to facts, and amenable only to subjective constructions imposed upon the facts? Collingwood's answer is in the negative: of the two, A and B, one is right, and the other wrong; which is to say that one of them has knowledge of the fact – C's action – while the other does not. The one who is in error is not placing an erroneous construction on a known fact; he is simply ignorant of the fact itself.

Thus the distinction between fact and the construction put upon it is false; what we call construction is merely our attempt to determine further details about the fact. And since the question of whether C was acting selfishly or not is a question of historical fact, the doctrine that people act in general selfishly or altruistically is based entirely on historical fact, or on something erroneously imagined to be historical fact.[7]

In other words, just as the mind cannot be studied in abstraction from the object of its attention, so a theoretical construction cannot be abstracted from the fact which it purports to interpret. In the context of *Religion and Philosophy*, Collingwood is concerned to exclude two kinds of view, both of which he considers irrationalist: one is the above-mentioned psychologism of James, the other is the radical historicism of Croce. While James held that the religious mind can be studied without raising such questions as whether God exists, Croce held that the history of ideas not only can, but must, study the development of ideas without raising the question of their truth or falsity. Both, according to Collingwood, attempted to study the life of the mind while ignoring the essential function of the mind, namely the critical function. The business of the mind is precisely to judge of truth and falsity, and a 'science of mind' which ignores this function sheds no light on what is supposed to be its subject: 'the mind, regarded in this external way, really ceases to be a mind at all.'[8]

Against both these approaches, Collingwood argues that no mental activity can be studied unless, at the same time, one also studies the object of that activity, i.e. engages in the very activity which one is studying. Once again, I think this must be taken in a narrowly rationalist or intellectualist sense; the presumption seems to be that the mental activity in question is a *rational* activity. Otherwise, we could not simply equate the study of the object of the activity with the actual engagement in the activity itself. (To clarify this point: the rather widespread assumption that the religious attitude is by nature irrational is one which Collingwood explicitly rejects; the whole book may be seen as an argument for the inherent rationality of Christianity.) Taken this way, Collingwood's argument implies concretely that such intellectual activities as the psychology of religion, the history of philosophy or of science, or the philosophy of history or of science, cannot be regarded as purely second-level studies; they must include within them also the first-level studies which form their subject-matter. Here Collingwood clearly disavows the approach of 'analytical philsophy', understood as a strictly second-level study of language, or of the methods of history or science. The purely analytical study of *methods* is, in Collingwood's view, impossible unless combined with the study of whether those methods yield real *knowledge*, something which cannot be settled a priori, but which entails the actual engagement in the type of thought concerned.

3. The theory of error does not seem to be seriously tackled in Collingwood's first book. If what we call an 'erroneous construction' of a fact is simply the failure to know the fact, then there seems to be no difference, in general, between error and ignorance. In *Religion and Philosophy*, there is no satisfactory account of the nature of error, a shortcoming which Collingwood, however, sought to make up for in his second published book, *Speculum Mentis* (1924).

Before leaving *Religion and Philosophy*, two main conclusions can be summed up: firstly, thoughts are public and objective, not private and subjective; secondly, the realm of thought cannot be stratified, in the sense that any intellectual activity can have for its object *merely* another intellectual activity, in complete abstraction from the first-order basis of facts (nor, on the other hand, can any study be *purely* factual and atheoretical; but that aspect need not now concern us).

In *Speculum Mentis*, Collingwood allows for a more sophisticated account of error, by introducing his distinction between knowing explicitly and knowing implicitly (a distinction dating back, in fact, to his lecture 'Ruskin's Philosophy' (1919), but absent from his very first book). In *Religion and Philosophy* Collingwood was led to equate religion, science, history, and philosophy as identical ways of knowing an identical object, the totality of facts. The borderlines ordinarily drawn between them he dismissed as a simple error – without, seemingly, leaving room for the possibility of such error. In *Speculum Mentis*, art, religion, science, history, and philosophy are arranged as a series of progressive steps of knowledge, each step explicating what was implicit on the step below. Thus what is explicitly art is implicitly religion, etc. Art is explicitly the suspension of judgement, that is, a form of supposal; this is what characterizes the questioning activity of the mind; a question is an assertion held in suspension. But this suspension cannot be sustained except as a kind of make-believe: a question which expects no answer is not a serious question; in this sense the question (or suspension of judgement) is implicitly an assertion. Art depicts symbolic images while suspending judgement as to their reality; religion asserts the reality of those images; what is known implicitly in art is known explicitly in religion. But assertion lays claim to truth and is therefore implicitly a question, the question about evidence; so religion is implicitly science, which supposes the existence of facts, which in turn are asserted by history. Philosophy, lastly, is the knowledge of what is known in art, religion, science, and history, *together with* the knowledge that precisely this is the manner in which it is known.

In this scheme, it is possible both to know and not to know the same object, by mistaking its explicit pretensions for its implicit nature. In this scheme, a stratification of intellectual activities is also clearly possible, but it is even more clearly seen to be an error, leading to the ossification of intellectual life. Thus the artist, the religious believer, the scientist, or the historian who perceives only the explicit pretensions of his endeavors becomes a dogmatic ideologue; he becomes an aestheticist, religious fanatic, positivist, or historicist. Likewise, the philosopher who attempts a second-level study of these endeavors, taking their explicit pretensions at face value, becomes an equally dogmatic 'formalist', with no understanding of the dynamisms inherent in the activities he is purporting to study:

> ... in all these dogmatisms there is a distinction between the direct form of consciousness (art, religion, etc.) and the reflective form (aestheticism, theism, etc.), and this appears as the distinction between direct or primary experience, as the apprehension of the object, and reflective or secondary experience, as the return of the mind upon itself to study its own primary experience. Such a distinction between primary and secondary experience is the infallible mark of dogmatism in all its varieties.[9]

In short, the gravest shortcoming of *Religion and Philosophy* — the lack of a theory of error — is now remedied, while the fundamental conclusions of the earlier book are left unimpaired, and even strengthened. Without a doubt, *Speculum Mentis* is, in its turn, open to criticism; its account of the epistemic status of philosophy, in particular, has met with something less than universal approval. But this need not concern us in the present context; the only point in the preceding has been to present Collingwood's early monistic philosophy of mind in a reasonably coherent and intelligible form, not to debate its truth or falsity. The need for such a presentation arises from the circumstance that his mature philosophy of history is couched, largely, in mentalistic terms, the meaning of which can be gathered only from the early writings. Anyone reading *The Idea of History* as an isolated work is likely to interpret the central notion of 're-enactment' in terms of an intuitive, commonsensical dualism, an interpretation which would make Collingwood out to be a sort of second-rate Dilthey. The objective of the above presentation is to pave the way for showing the inappropriateness of such an interpretation.

8. The Theory of Presuppositions I:
An Interpretation

The reason why there is no urgent need to defend or to criticize Collingwood's early philosophy of mind is that its central conclusions were later reformulated by him within an entirely different set of parameters, in the theory of presuppositions expounded in *An Autobiography* and *An Essay on Metaphysics*.

Briefly, the theory is this. A sensible and intelligent statement is never merely an assertion made *in vacuo*; it is always at the same time the answer to a definite question. The question, in its turn, is never simply tossed out of nowhere; if it is a serious question, it has to arise from a set of (logically) prior presuppositions. These, in turn, are statements, and are consequently the answers to prior questions, and so forth. An intellectual tradition is made up of such a chain of questions and answers, each answer serving as a presupposition – or a 'logical ground' – for the next question. The analysis of an intellectual tradition therefore consists in relating a body of statements to the questions to which the statements serve as the answers, and uncovering the tacit and hidden presuppositions from which those questions have arisen. Only so can we achieve historical understanding of the tradition and of our own relation to it.

This approach to historical interpretation can be illustrated with an example from Collingwood's *The Idea of Nature*, from the chapter on ancient Greek cosmology. Thales was the first in recorded history to ask the question 'What is nature?', and to him the question meant 'What kind of thing is nature made of?', on the presupposition that nature is itself made of one of the kinds of stuff of which things *in* nature are made. The answer he arrived at was 'Water'. For a variety of reasons, this answer seemed unsatisfactory to his successor Anaximander, who repeated the question, but whose answer shows that the question was now given a different twist. Nature, according to Anaximander, is made of 'apeiron', an undifferentiated something. The answer shows that his question was not quite the same as that of Thales; when asking what nature is made of, Anaximander was not looking for the kind of stuff which things *in* nature are made of, but something different in kind. This presupposition of the qualitative difference between nature itself and things in nature raised a novel question. The question now arose as to how nature, and *eo ipso* the things in nature, could be made of something qualitatively different from the stuff we find in nature. The emergence of this new presuppositon and the new problem-situation is crucial for understanding Anaximander's successor Anaximenes. When the latter again raised the question 'What is nature?' and answered 'Vapor', he might seem to be returning to the problem-situation of Thales, by focusing on a stuff found in nature. But this appearance is illusory; the question, properly understood, is a different one from that of Thales. Anaximenes has inherited from Anaximander the problem of how things come into being, and the question of the raw material is now subsidiary to the question of the process of generation. Vapor is chosen because, unlike apeiron, it is obviously malleable to condensation and rarefaction, and so accounts for both the raw material and the process. And so on. The answer given by each generation serves as the presupposition on the basis of which a new question arises; by hindsight, the process is a continuous and progressive chain of questions and answers.

For our purposes, the theory of presuppositions may usefully be presented in juxtaposition with Collingwood's earlier philosophy of mind. As we recall, there were, in the earlier works, two essential conclusions:

1) Intellectual life cannot be stratified, i.e. an intellectual activity cannot have for its object another intellectual activity without including the latter within itself, as part of its activity, not merely as its subject-matter.

2) The possibility of 1) is provided for by the essentially public character of thought, which ensures the accessibility and, as it were, transparency of all those systems of thought of which we have knowledge.

In terms of the theory of presuppositions, 1) can be paraphrased as follows:

I) The intellectual import of a statement can be understood only when it is understood what the question is to which the statement is an answer.

II) The question can be reconstructed only by reconstructing the entire problem-situation, or 'set of presuppositions', which gave rise to the question, and which gave the question its precise force or impact.

III) The only way of reconstructing the precise force of the question, and hence of the answer, from the set of presuppositions, is by actually making those presuppositions, seriously raising the question, and seriously attempting to answer it.

Paragraph 2) can then be paraphrased:

IV) When our contemporaries make presuppositions which are alien to ours, we can uncover them because the realm of such presuppositions is bounded by a common human rationality, every corner of which can be invaded, given sufficient imagination and goodwill.

V) The presuppositons made by previous generations are accessible to us because our own presuppositions are linked with theirs through a continuous chain of questions and answers. We can reconstruct this chain by construing our own presuppositons as the answers to prior questions, and so forth.

These theses were advanced by Collingwood as an attempted synthesis, intended to solve chiefly two problems with which he was perennially occupied: that of philosophical argument and that of historical explanation. In both cases, he concluded, the proper method lies in the reconstruction of alien presuppositional frameworks, and in the asking and answering of the questions arising from those frameworks. This is, in its barest outlines, Collingwood's theory of presuppositions or, if one wishes, his version of 'situational analysis'. So far, I have sketched the theory using my own words, which are different from Collingwood's. I shall now cover the same ground in more detail, noting my interpretations of Collingwood, where I have found him either unclear or inconsistent, and points of disagreement with him, where I have found him to be mistaken.

I have here interpreted Collingwood's theory of presuppositions as a theory of the *intellectual import* of statements, i.e. essentially as a hermeneutic; Collingwood himself *also* presents it as a) a method of discovery, b) a theory of logic, and c) a theory of meaning. On all three counts, I find the explicit pretensions either unfulfilled or fulfilled only trivially.

a) Collingwood claims to have derived what he calls his 'Logic of Question and Answer' from two sources: from his own experience of archeological research, and from the methodological teachings of Bacon and Descartes. In archeological research he learnt that one learns something from an excavation only to the extent that one approaches it with precise and definite questions in mind; with the attitude, 'let's dig and see what we find', one learns nothing, except accidentally. In digging, one has to be on the look-out for objects of a particular kind, namely, such objects as may serve as evidence in relation to a specific hypothesis or question. This practical experience seemed to corroborate Bacon's and Descartes's injunctions to devise controlled experiments and 'put Nature to the question':

> Here I was only rediscovering for myself, in the practice of historical research, principles which Bacon and Descartes had stated, three hundred years earlier, in connexion with the natural sciences. Each of them had said very plainly that knowledge comes only by asking questions, and that these questions must be the right questions and asked in the right order.[1]

Leaving aside the question of the appropriateness of lumping together Bacon and Descartes in this way, the general observation on the nature of research is perfectly proper and not entirely trivial. But it is much too weak to carry the philosophical weight which Collingwood wishes subsequently to place on it. From the statement that we learn only by asking precise questions in a methodical manner, nothing whatever follows about what questions we should ask. It certainly does not follow – as Collingwood concludes in the case of historical research – that *we* should ask the questions asked by *the historical agents*. The 'logic' of question and answer is logically quite unsupported by Collingwood's observations regarding either his archeological experience or the Baconian method. It is another matter that, once one has arrived at Collingwood's 'logic' – the view of historical research as the uncovering of questions asked, and presuppositions made, by the agents – one is likely to become acutely aware of the role played by one's own questions and presuppositions in the practice of one's research. In his autobiographical account, Collingwood seems to put the cart before the horse; and one is led to suspect that he did, in fact, first arrive at his theory of presuppositions and then invent a suitable autobiographical story accounting for its origins. This may sound unkind, but it would be far more unkind to assume that he derived his theory from the methodological observations, from which nothing remotely like the theory actually follows.

b) In *An Autobiography* (1939), Collingwood proclaims a 're-volution in logic'; specifically, he claims that topics like 'truth' and 'contradiction' cannot be satisfactorily accounted for within the framework of propositional logic, but only within that of his own analysis of question and answer.

With regard to contradiction, the claim is that we cannot know two propositions to be contradictory unless we know their meaning, and we cannot know their meaning unless we know the respective questions which they attempt to answer. Collingwood states his major premise boldly: 'No two propositions . . . can contradict one another unless they are the answers to the same question.'[2] Taken literally, this seems to be simply false, although the weaker claim seems to be true, that no two propositions can be contradictory unless they are the answers to the same *type* of question, i.e. unless they belong on the same level of meaning. (To be exact, this would seem true of *sentences*, not of *propositions*.) This has been generally appreciated by formal logicians; it represents a real problem, which has been tackled more or less successfully, e.g. by Russell in the *Theory of Types*. But the problem is misstated by Collingwood; what is involved is the *semantical* problem of identifying the two propositions given two seemingly contradictory sentences; it is not the case that, *given* two propositions, a further problem arises. The distinction is clearly exhibited in a formal calculus, where the problem is entirely eliminated from the calculus by stipulations as to the domain of the quantifiers. So the problem is not the *logical* one of detecting contradictions between propositions, but the *semantical* one of how to identify propositions. This shifts the burden to the theory of meaning (cf. c) below).

Similar considerations apply to the discussion of truth. Specifically, Collingwood claims that a proposition cannot be true unless it forms the answer to a question which arises from presuppositions which have, in fact, been made, i.e. a serious question. The condition is that 'the question is what we ordinarily call a sensible or intelligent question, not a silly one, or in my terminology it "arises" '.[3] This, too, seems to be literally false; it is true that I am not now sitting in an aeroplane, although that is not the answer to any question which, in

Collingwood's sense, can be said to 'arise' in the present situation. (One possible question might be: 'What is an example of a true proposition?', but then the proposition would have to be put in quotes and suffixed '. . . is an example of a true proposition.') Once again, Collingwood's observation would be true in a weaker version, but not one which would yield his conclusion. It is true, as has been remarked upon by Frege and Strawson, that we should not raise the question of the truth or falsity of a statement which was not seriously made; but it does not follow that the proposition (or sentence) used in making the statement might not *be* either true or false. It would have to be independently argued that this is an illegitimate use of the terms 'true' and 'false'. Be that as it may, if we substitute this weaker version the burden is once more shifted to the theory of meaning: Collingwood would have to make good the claim that the serious assertion of a proposition is tantamount to answering a serious question.

In both cases, then, Collingwood's statements about logic are seen to be indefensible as they stand; when reformulated as statements about meaning they are at least debatable; with this move, however, position b) collapses into c).

c) In his *Autobiography*, Collingwood makes this claim:

. . . you cannot find out what a man means by simply studying his spoken or written statements, even though he has spoken or written with perfect command of the language and with perfectly truthful intention. In order to find out his meaning you must also know what the question was (a question in his mind, and presumed by him to be in yours) to which the thing he has said or written was meant as an answer.[4]

In the later *Essay on Metaphysics*, the analogous claim is made more simply, 'Every statement that anybody ever makes is made in answer to a question.'[5] And the question is not here presumed by anyone to be in anyone's mind: 'In proportion as a man is thinking scientifically when he makes a statement, he knows that his statement is the answer to a question and knows what the question is. In proportion as he is thinking unscientifically he does not know these things.'[6] (In Collingwood's terminology, 'scientifically' stands for 'methodically'.)

For purposes of analyzing Collingwood's theory of meaning, we may distinguish between two uses of the term 'meaning', which are frequently found in the current literature on semantics:

i) That which the speaker intends to communicate on a particular occasion of utterance; i.e. the 'occasion-meaning' or 'utterer's meaning' discussed in the writings of Strawson and Grice.[7]

ii) The set of rules which permit the speaker's intention to be conventionally realized in a set of physical symbols. To discover the 'meaning' of a sentence, in this sense, means to discover the *range* of intentions which the rules permit to be realized in the one sentence. This is the type of meaning discussed in the speech-act semantics of Austin and Searle,[8] as well as in the 'generative semantics' of Chomsky.[9]

In both cases we distinguish, following Frege, between the publicly communicable meaning, or sense, and the private associative net of ideas connected with the sense in the mind of any one individual speaker. Since Collingwood rather emphatically disavows any intention of doing psychology, we can take it, I think, that he would accept this distinction.

In *An Autobiography* (cf. quote on p. 76, above) Collingwood seems to be concerned with meaning i), i.e. the conscious intention to communicate something definite on a particular occasion. In *An Essay on Metaphysics*, however, this concern is, as we have seen, quite explicitly disavowed. Even within the former work the position is ambiguous. We recall that Collingwood claims to be speaking about the kind of meaning which one needs to know in order to determine the truth of a proposition, or the logical relations between propositions. Now truth-conditions depend on linguistic context and (sometimes, though not always) on the extra-linguistic conditions of utterance, on the particular occasion. Occasion-meaning is relevant notably in the case of sentences containing demonstratives or personal pronouns; here we do have to know the intended reference, on the particular occasion of utterance, in order to determine the truth-conditions. But it is not generally the case that we can simply intend a statement to have these truth-conditions rather than those. The statement 'William the Conqueror landed at Hastings in 1066' becomes none the less true for being offered as the (wrong) answer to the question 'Who was the first English king to land on the coast of Yorkshire?'[10] Of course, anyone so answering that question, intends

'Hastings' to refer to some place on the coast of Yorkshire, but that intention, or any other conditions of utterance, do not in the least affect the truth-conditions of the statement. From the recognition of the (wider or narrower) context-dependency of truth-conditions, it does not follow either that the relevant context can be simply intended into being, or that knowledge of a speaker's intention, or of any other conditions of a *particular utterance* of a statement, is always required for determining the truth-conditions of that statement.

If Collingwood were propounding a theory of meaning in the sense of i), it would be a false one; and this he seems to recognize in *An Essay on Metaphysics*. The question does not have to be in the speaker's mind; in fact, it is there only when he is thinking in a methodical fashion; in the sloppy thinking typical of most people most of the time there is usually no awareness of any question being asked. Still, every statement is the answer to a precise question. How so? Because to every question there is one and only one right answer; conversely, to every statement there is one and only one question to which it is the right answer. How do we discover the question? By analyzing the presuppositions that have been made; presuppositions are endowed with something called 'logical efficacy', which causes certain definite questions to 'arise'. To take one of Collingwood's examples, someone who asks me whether I have stopped beating my wife yet may not *know* that he is presupposing both that I have a wife and that I have been in the habit of beating her. Nonetheless, if I am to take the question as a sensible one, I must assume that, consciously or not, he has in fact made those presuppositions. Now, I do not think there is anything counter-intuitive about the notion of someone presupposing something without the presupposition being 'in his mind', either consciously or subconsciously. In ordinary discussion, when a man is told 'You are assuming something', he is prepared (if he is a reasonable man) to be told what he is assuming, and he does not expect a psychoanalysis but a reconstruction of the assumption by inference from his explicit statements. The idea of the 'logical efficacy' of presuppositions is not, I believe, in itself a controversial one; the questionable, or ambiguous, claim is that the *meaning* of questions and their answers depends on this logical efficacy.

We have seen that this claim cannot be defended if we take 'meaning' in sense (i), and we have also seen that, in the *Essay*, Collingwood explicitly precludes this interpretation. Neither, however, is it to be taken in sense (ii), as is clear from the following passage: 'A question that "does not arise" is thus a nonsense question: not intrinsically nonsensical, but nonsensical in relation to its context, and specifically to its presuppositions.'[11] 'Intrinsically nonsensical' clearly corresponds to nonsensical in our sense (ii) of meaning; that is, nonsensical relative to the broad 'context' provided simply by the rules of the language. But Collingwood is talking about nonsense and meaning relative to a context narrower than (ii) yet broader than that provided by the particular occasion of utterance, as in (i). His notion of 'meaning' does not, therefore, fall within either of the two semantic categories considered, the narrow one of 'occasion-meaning', or the broader one of 'significance'. My suggestion is that Collingwood is not really concerned with 'meaning' in any sense recognized by empirical semantics; rather, he is talking about what I have called 'intellectual import' i.e. the 'force' of a statement in relation to, say, the development of an argument, the state of a discussion, or a particular literary or scientific tradition. In other words, his theory of 'meaning' is, as already suggested, a theory of interpretation in the hermeneutic tradition from Dilthey to Gadamer.

If Collingwood is really speaking of historical interpretation, why does he purport to speak of truth, logic, and meaning? I think this misleading choice of terminology must be attributed to a desire to gain a hearing in the positivistic atmosphere of Oxford in the thirties. Collingwood's intellectual isolation in this environment was striking. When *Speculum Mentis* was published, it was described by a reviewer as 'the same old Idealist nonsense'. When *An Essay on Philosophical Method* appeared in 1933, it was reviewed by Gilbert Ryle, who claimed that he could not 'make head or tail of it', and anyone reading Ryle's review will find this admission both honest and truthful. Collingwood clearly perceived that the perspective of contemporary Oxford orthodoxy distorted his thought by making it appear as old-fashioned idealism – an idealism, by the way, which his Oxford contemporaries were sadly ignorant of. It is my belief, however, that Collingwood's self-conscious attempt at overcoming this barrier may prove equally distorting if his explicit pretensions are taken at face value. The recovery of what is of value in his works requires, therefore, a certain ruthlessness in criticizing his explicit statements.

9. The Theory of Presuppositions II: Critical Reservations

In the previous chapter I was concerned with criticizing Colling-wood's formulation of his theory for the purposes of interpretation. In this chapter I feel obliged to take exception to the theory on two questions of substance, rather than of mere formulation. These are 1) the linear ordering of presuppositions; 2) the theory of absolute presuppositions.

1) Most questions involve several presuppositions, e.g. in the case of 'Have you stopped beating your wife yet?', where the presuppositions are both that you have a wife, and that you have been in the habit of beating her — and, perhaps, that you have formed the intention to stop, or at least that you are expected to form that intention. In such a case, Collingwood holds, the presuppositions are made in a particular linear order, each presupposition answering a question arising from the previous one. It is only the last presupposition in the line that counts as *the* presupposition of the explicit question, comprising, as it were, the whole line of previous presuppositions within it. It is Collingwood's general contention that all our thought can — and should — be analyzed on this pattern: each proposition uniquely answering one question, each question uniquely arising from one presupposition, which in turn answers one and only one question, and so forth. The claim is not only that this is how we think *when* we think methodically, but that this is the structure which we shall discover whenever we analyze any piece of thought methodically.

I want here to make two observations, one general and one more particular.

In the first place, it is true that when we analyze a piece of thought rationally and methodically it will itself appear more rational and methodical than it would otherwise. This is so because, in a certain sense, it is only rational thought that *can* be reconstructed rationally;

for the purpose of such analysis we adopt a presumption of rationality and 'reconstruct' irrationality only negatively, as a deviation from the presumed norm of rationality. This notion is certainly not peculiar to Collingwood; Max Weber, for instance, argued convincingly that even irrational phenomena such as panics on the stock exchange can be characterized rationally only as a series of deviations from a presumed norm.[1]

In the second place, though, it is far from clear that Collingwood's schema represents the essence of rational, or even methodical, thought. The stringent linear ordering of presuppositions, with its one-to-one correspondence between question and presupposition, seems to fit his own chosen example but counter-examples are not hard to come by. Take the question, 'Why did a conservative like Nixon institute price controls?'. There are three presuppositions, that Nixon is a conservative, that he has instituted price controls, and that the event of a conservative instituting price controls is something calling for a special explanation. These three presuppositions are separately necessary and jointly sufficient for the question to 'arise' in Collingwood's sense. But I see no natural way of arranging them on a linear ordering as prescribed by Collingwood; no one presupposition seems more immediate, or more proximate, than the others. Any one of the three may intelligibly be suspended, or fail to be presupposed, and the question will fail to arise. Nor do I think that the example is in any way contrived; it is a perfectly commonplace kind of question.

Of course, Collingwood does not claim that the linear ordering represents a temporal priority; he would not deny that we do, as a matter of fact, often make a cluster of presuppositions simultaneously. But he does claim that, for purposes of rational reconstruction, the cluster must be disentangled and the presuppositions arranged linearly, and that there is always one and only one order in which to arrange them. The attractiveness of this view is of course its alluring simplicity. While I think that for hermeneutical or pedagogical purposes it is sometimes desirable to adopt this linear order as a mode of presentation, still one adopts it at the risk of doing an injustice to the complexity of the progress of thought through discussion. Certainly, the presumption of rationality does not imply the presumption of a rigid and single-minded investigation; such investigations are rarely met with in the history of science, to say nothing of other branches of human thought.

However, although I think that the idea of a unique correlation between questions and presuppositions must be discarded, we must not miss the important point which Collingwood here makes in an, as usual, exaggerated form, namely that a set of presuppositions, while permitting certain questions to be raised, at the same time *excludes* a vast range of questions from arising, thereby barring entire problem areas from discussion. To analyze this phenomenon with a minimum of rigor one has to give some subsets of presuppositions priority over others, in order of discussion. This seems to be the kernel of truth in Collingwood's overstated claim. And even though this is a more modest claim, it is not for that reason entirely trivial.

2) In my initial sketch of the theory of presuppositions, I attributed the possibility of historical understanding to the essential continuity in the chain of presuppositions. I think this presumption of continuity is essential in order to avoid altogether skeptical conclusions. Collingwood clearly disavows any inclination toward skepticism; yet he equivocates on the all-important principle of continuity. For this reason he has been accused by among others W. H. Walsh and Stephen Toulmin[2] of becoming a sceptic *malgré lui*. Since Toulmin's criticism, in particular, is not dissimilar from my own criticism of Popper, it is incumbent on me to show how Collingwood's theory can be rendered immune to such criticism – admittedly at the cost of revision.

The principle of continuity is most clearly stated in *An Essay on Philosophical Method* (1933): 'the entire history of thought is the history of a single sustained attempt to solve a single problem, each phase advancing the problem by the extent of all the work done on it in the interval, and summing up the fruits of this work in the shape of a unique presentation of the problem.'[3] The principle is re-stated in *An Autobiography*, in a discussion of the connection between Plato's *Republic* and Hobbes's *Leviathan*: 'The sameness is the sameness of an historical process, and the difference is the difference between one thing which in the course of that process has turned into something else, and the other thing into which it has turned. Plato's *polis* and Hobbes's absolute State are related *by a traceable historical process*, whereby one has turned into the other . . .'[4] (My italics) On the other hand, in *The Idea of Nature* (posthumous, 1945), Collingwood seeks to analyze the history of cosmology as a continuous progression of questions and answers; but the analysis breaks down at certain crucial points, and what Collingwood actually presents is the merely temporal succession of three apparently discontinuous 'ideas of nature', where continuity obtains only *within* each of the three. In *An Essay on Metaphysics,* Collingwood seems *prima facie* to re-affirm this discontinuity by introducing the notion of 'absolute presuppositions', in contrast to 'relative presuppositions'. The two notions are defined as follows:

> By a relative presupposition I mean one which stands relatively to one question as its presupposition and relatively to another question as its answer.
>
> An absolute presupposition is one which stands, relatively to all questions to which it is related, as a presupposition, never as an answer.[5]

Since *every* proposition is the answer to a question, it follows that absolute presuppositions, such as 'God exists' or 'Every event has a cause', are not propositions. They cannot be true or false, and they cannot therefore be criticized or justified. Metaphysics, according to Collingwood, is the 'science of absolute presuppositions'; it is a purely historical science, whose task is simply to ascertain what absolute presuppositions were made by what culture at what time. The further task of criticizing or justifying absolute presuppositions is not the domain of metaphysics proper, but of pseudo-metaphysics, which is based on a confusion of absolute presuppositions with propositions.

Collingwood is here attempting to defend metaphysics against A. J. Ayer's onslaught in *Language, Truth and Logic.* The ambiguous defence consists in austerely limiting the pretensions of metaphysical statements so as to make them pass both the analytic–empirical distinction and the verifiability test. Ayer's attack, according to Collingwood, is based on a confusion of metaphysics proper, which is entirely verifiable through historical research, with pseudo-metaphysics, which is both unverifiable and nonsensical. One obvious question is, of course: How many traditional metaphysical systems can be said to pass Collingwood's test? For our purposes, however, there are more urgent questions. If absolute presuppositions are neither criticizable nor justifiable, how can the historian-metaphysician deal with them except in terms of mere temporal succession? How can this succession possibly be exhibited as a rational progression? What happens to the principle of the essential continuity of the development of human thought if the rational reconstruction of that development must inevitably come to an absolute halt as soon as it reaches an absolute presupposition? As we recall, historical reconstruction consists in connecting answers with questions, but absolute presuppositions are defined as not being the answers to any questions; how, then, can their origins be accounted for in terms of Collingwood's theory of interpretation?

From a reading of *An Essay on Metaphysics,* two conclusions emerge: In the first place, Collingwood nowhere seriously confronts these questions; in the second place, he does not confront them because he does not perceive any inconsistency between the principle of continuity and the theory of absolute presuppositions. Only in a footnote does Collingwood address himself, briefly, to the question of why absolute presuppositions change. Here, he replies to a friend who 'thinks readers may credit me with the opinion that such changes are merely "changes of fashion" '. Collingwood's answer shows an astounding lack of self-consciousness: 'Why, asks my friend, do such changes happen? Briefly, because the absolute presuppositions of any given society, at any given phase of its history, form a structure which is subject to "strains" of greater or less intensity, which are "taken up" in various ways, but never annihilated. If the strains are too great, the structure collapses and is replaced by another, which will be a modification of the old with the destructive strain removed; a modification not consciously devised but created by a process of unconscious thought.'[6]

If we seriously follow up this suggestion, it will not take us many steps before we shall have obliterated the distinction between absolute and relative presuppositions. The notion of 'strain', it turns out, is conceptually connected with the logical notion of contradiction, so it is a *critical* notion, not a merely descriptive one. Roughly, a constellation of presuppositions is under 'strain' when different presuppositions give rise to questions which receive mutually contradictory answers. To describe the collapse of such a structure thus amounts to judging that its strain was too great, i.e. that the structure was too incoherent or too irrational. In short, to describe its collapse amounts to criticizing the structure, with the implication that the structure itself is the answer to a question or a cluster of questions. To describe the emergence of a new structure, free from that particular strain, is to describe a more coherent or more rational structure; to that extent it amounts to justifying the new structure, with the same implication as above.

In an earlier work on Collingwood, I attempted to give a re-interpretation of the theory of absolute presuppositions so as to make it consistent with the principle of continuity.[7] I am no longer entirely satisfied with this argument and although I do not wish to retract it, I also do not wish to let anything for present purposes depend on an argument which, I fear, may fail to carry conviction. For the purposes of the present discussion, I should put the matter as follows. Collingwood's theory of the historical understanding is self-contained without the theory of absolute presuppositions. The latter theory was introduced by Collingwood for the quite different purpose of defending metaphysics against the attacks from logical positivists. Even for that purpose, the theory of absolute presuppositions was hardly required: as is now widely agreed, logical positivism is, in most of its versions, self-refuting. But it seems, in *An Essay on Metaphysics*, that Collingwood has not seriously considered the possibility that people might take him to be a skeptic or a relativist. His objective in this book is to combat Ayer's skepticism, and his chief concern is apparently to make it clear that he himself is not the apriorist that Ryle had taken him to be and that Ayer might take him to be. For this purpose, and quite needlessly, Collingwood accepts both the analytic–empirical dichotomy and the verification principle. Within this set of parameters the principle of continuity cannot even be intelligibly stated. Once again, if my reading is correct, Collingwood goes wrong because of a self-conscious effort to express himself in a language sufficiently stultifying to be understood by his contemporary Oxford colleagues.

What, after these criticisms, remains of Collingwood's theory of presuppositions? Roughly, the positions I outlined in paragraphs I) to V) in the last chapter. History is not a hypothetico-deductive science, where the facts can be neatly divided from our hypotheses about the facts. Human history can be reconstructed rationally and so rendered intelligible to the extent that it can be reconstructed as attempts at rationally solving problems, which we are able to grasp to the extent that we are able to entertain the presuppositions on which those problems have arisen. The possibility of such reconstruction is afforded by the continuity of an intellectual tradition: by uncovering our own presuppositions and questioning them, we can discover the questions occupying the previous generation, and so on. It is only by traversing this intellectual tradition – seriously making the presuppositions made by previous generations and thereby making their problems our own — that we can attain an understanding of distant ages, making them, in our imagination, our contemporaries. To the extent that this reconstruction is impossible, the writing of history is impossible.

Furthermore – and, perhaps, most importantly – to the extent that the writing of history is possible, it is possible because this rational reconstruction does not presume to penetrate the veil of private emotions, affections, or sensations. The idea that presuppositions may be made and questions asked without anybody being aware of it, entails that thoughts lead a life of their own, independently of this or that thinking subject. In other words, the object of reconstruction is the purely intellectual content of thought, not the emotive processes in which the content is embedded. Collingwood's idea of the 'logical efficacy' of presuppositions expresses something very much like Frege's idea of a thought which is not in anybody's mind, and which constitutes the stuff of which intellectual traditions are made. Since Collingwood does not presuppose any stratification of the realm of thought, this Fregean idea does not here generate the problems we encountered in our discussion of Popper.

10. The Re-Enactment of the Past

Among the many ideas of considerable interest contained in *The Idea of History*, I wish to single out the controversial idea of history as the 're-enactment' of past thought. In this chapter I intend to do three things. First, I shall place the idea of re-enactment explicitly within the parameters of the monistic philosophy of mind, which I think Collingwood at this stage presupposed. Secondly, I shall offer a criticism of this idea, and thirdly, I shall argue that this criticism constitutes a reason for considering the theory of presuppositions, rather than the notion of re-enactment, as the most mature and most defensible version of Collingwood's theory of historical explanation.

The idea of 're-enactment' is this: every rational, and hence intelligible, action performed by an historical ageat has an intellectual content. The agent was faced with a problem, and his action was his attempt to solve that problem. The problem can be expressed as a question, and the action embodies a particular answer. In reconstructing an historical event, the historian must ask the question that confronted the agent and reconstruct his answer to that question. Now, according to Collingwood's monistic philosophy of mind, the assertive content of a thought cannot, even for purposes of analysis, be separated from the act of thinking that thought. It is granted that, say, Euclid's postulates have an objective thought-content, but in grasping that content I actually perform Euclid's act of thinking, not an act 'like' it but that very same act. The subject-act-object monism of Collingwood's earlier writings is already familiar to us, and the present contention should cause no confusion from the point of view of the philosophy of mind there set forth. But it may seem objectionable on common-sense grounds to hold that the same act of thought can be performed by two persons separated in time by two thousand years. Now Collingwood tries to show that this idea cannot really be controverted on common-sense grounds. Suppose a person thinks for five seconds, 'the angles are equal'. Is he performing one act, sustained over five seconds, or is he performing a succession of acts and, if the latter, how many? Clearly, any number assigned would be quite arbitrary, and it seems the only sensible thing to say that there is a single act, sustained over five seconds.

Then consider a slightly different case.

Suppose that, after thinking 'the angles are equal' for five seconds, the thinker allows his attention to wander for three more; and then, returning to the same subject, again thinks 'the angles are equal'. Have we here two acts of thought and not one, because a time elapsed between them? Clearly not; there is one single act, this time not merely sustained, but revived after an interval. For there is no difference in this case that was not already present in the other. When an act is sustained over five seconds, the activity in the fifth second is just as much separated from that in the first, as when the intervening seconds are occupied by an activity of a different kind or (if that be possible) by none.[1]

The argument is that on common-sense grounds one and the same act may be sustained over time, but this means that two phases of the same act may be separated by an interval. Whether that interval be three seconds or two thousand years is, in Collingwood's view, a matter of degree and not of principle, and is, therefore, of no fundamental importance.

Here, of course, common sense may raise the objection that the unity of the act sustained over time, or revived after an interval, is provided for by the unity of the thinking mind, so that although I can at successive moments perform one and the same act of thought, I cannot perform the acts of a different mind, such as Euclid's. Collingwood's answer would be to ask common sense for a satisfactory theory of personal identity. On his own theory, as we have seen, the unity of a single mind is constituted by the totality of its activities. The thought-content 'the angles are equal' requires for its comprehension one and only one mental act appropriate to it. If Euclid thought it, and I am thinking it, then I am performing the same mental act as Euclid and, to precisely that extent, I am Euclid. The unity of the mind is provided by the unity of the act and the unity of the act is provided by the object thought about.

> The act of thinking, then, is not only subjective but objective as well. It is not only a thinking, it is something that can be thought about. But, because ... it is never merely objective, it requires to be thought about in a peculiar way, a way only appropriate to itself. ... It can never be studied 'objectively', in the sense in which 'objectively' excludes 'subjectively'. It has to be studied as it actually exists, that is to say, as an act. And because this act is subjectivity (though not mere subjectivity) or experience, it can be studied only in its own subjective being, that is, by the thinker whose activity or experience it is.[2]

The implications for historical knowledge are made quite explicit: 'Historical knowledge is the knowledge of what the mind has done in the past, and at the same time it is the redoing of this, the perpetuation of past acts in the present. Its object is therefore not a mere object, something outside the mind which knows it; it is an activity of thought, which can be known only in so far as the knowing mind re-enacts it and knows itself as so doing.'[3] Premising that all thinking is essentially an activity and, conversely, all action inherently intellectual, Collingwood generalizes from the history of thought to all history. The actions of a Caesar or a Napoleon, in so far as they are intelligible, are thoughts as well as actions. Caesar and Napoleon were confronted by problem-situations embodying questions, and the actions by which they sought to solve their problems are the answers to those questions. In writing about Caesar or Napoleon, what the historian tries to do is to ask and answer their questions; that is, to think their thoughts and, to just that extent, actually to be Caesar or Napoleon. In this sense the past which the historian investigates is a living past constituted by thoughts which are his own; and in this sense Collingwood is ready to endorse Croce's notorious dictum, that 'all history is contemporary history'.[4]

It is easy to misconstrue this theory – as Popper does – as a theory of the empathetic identification with another subject. Collingwood's theory lends itself to misinterpretation because he seeks to express in dualistic terms, such as 'subjective' and 'objective', a view which presupposes a monistic metaphysics, in which the subject–object distinction is obliterated. Collingwood's view is that a ratiocinative process can be made an object of thought only by being actually repeated. In dualistic terms this conception can be expressed only by saying that thoughts are both objective and subjective: they have an objective content which can be shared by several thinkers, but this content can be grasped only subjectively; that is, if I wish to grasp the thoughts of someone else, I must grasp them in just the same way as he does. What is misleading is the fact that the word 'subjective' carries overtones of 'private emotive processes'. It is already clear from our reading of *Religion and Philosophy* that the acts of which Collingwood is speaking are purely ratiocinative processes which are, in his view, as public as the objects of thought. This point is further elaborated in *The Idea of History*, where Collingwood explains how he can appropriate the thoughts expressed in Plato's *Theatetus* without knowing the entire situation in which Plato thought those thoughts:

> In Plato's mind, this existed in a certain context of discussion and theory; in my mind, because I do not know that context, it exists in a different one, namely that of the discussion arising out of modern sensationalism. Because it is a thought and not a mere feeling or sensation, it can exist in both these contexts without losing its identity, although without some appropriate context it could not exist.[5]

The above completes my refutation of Popper's interpretation of Collingwood, a misinterpretation based in part, admittedly, on a certain obscurity inherent in Collingwood's mentalistic terminology. But there is another, more serious way in which Collingwood's mentalistic approach vitiates what I have taken to be the crux of his theory of historical understanding, and that is his postulation of a one-to-one correspondence between thought-contents and acts of thought. This one-to-one correspondence is essential if the publicness of the object (hence of the content) of thought is to assure the publicness of the corresponding act. Even if we discard Popper's misinterpretation and construe 'mental act' in the strictly intellectualist sense which Collingwood intended, the one-to-one correspondence still does not seem to hold. The possession of, or commitment to, a propositional content just does not always seem to be an event having a temporal location, as for instance a speech-act is.

What, then, is a mental act? Recent philosophical literature contains two antithetical views on the ontological status of mental acts. On the one hand there is Ryle's view that statements of the occurrence of mental acts are disguised general statements, carrying counterfactual conditionals.[6] Opposed to this is P. T. Geach's view, derived from Thomas Aquinas (who has clearly also been a source of inspiration for Collingwood's early philosophy), that mental acts are instances of 'saying in one's heart', strictly analogous to speech-acts.[7] My own view is that we do sometimes perform temporally locatable mental acts (as I do now), but that these by no means exhaust the realm of thought. 'I have always thought that the earth is round': I have not been constantly engaged in a mental activity corresponding to the content of that thought. The statement of my having that thought is not a spatio-temporal singular statement, but a general statement, carrying counterfactual conditionals, and saying something, for instance, about what direction I should take were I to travel to Southeast Asia. Now this thought, that the earth is round, has the status of what Collingwood later calls a presupposition, i.e. a thought not necessarily 'in my mind', yet in a sense determining my explicit thoughts. The recognition of the existence of such thoughts runs counter to the one-to-one correspondence between thought-contents and acts of thought postulated in Collingwood's early philosophy; their existence, therefore, cannot be accounted for within that framework.

The early philosophy of mind – in terms of which the notion of re-enactment is couched – is accordingly narrower in scope than the later theory of presuppositions. The latter accounts for essential features of thought left unexplained by the former – but the converse does not seem true. In particular, with regard to the theory of historical knowledge, Collingwood's early monism does not seem to yield any essential conclusions which we did not find to follow from the theory of presuppositions. In methodological terms, the method of imaginatively re-enacting past thought *is* simply the method of presuppositional analysis outlined in *An Autobiography* and *An Essay on Metaphysics.* The difference lies in the question of the metaphysical presuppositions on which one justifies the method epistemologically. The minimum metaphysical requirement seems to be the recognition of the objectivity of thoughts, whether that objectivity be realized through an Aristotelian monism, Platonic dualism, or Fregean plural-ism. In *The Idea of History* the first alternative is adopted; in *An Essay on Metaphysics,* however, the ontological question is suspended and only the minimum requirement of objectivity is explicitly as-serted, although the language employed is suggestive of something like a Fregean pluralism, which is also the alternative which raises least problems.

11. Summary and Conclusion

Both Popper and Collingwood agree that historical explanations are not causal but rational explanations, in the sense explained in Chapter 1. Historical events are to be analyzed as complexes of individual human actions. 'Explaining' an event means exhibiting its rationality by analyzing the problem-situation from which it arose, and showing the action to constitute a reasonable or plausible response to a problem which the historian himself recognizes as a genuine one. Once these conditions are fulfilled — the problem is recognized as a genuine problem, and the action is recognized as a reasonable response to that problem — then the action is sufficiently explained in the sense that we understand it as something which was to be expected. This is the strongest explanation we can have of an historical event: that it is seen as fulfilling a reasonable expectation. We can never explain historical events causally, as something which was bound to happen and hence predictable from a given set of necessary and sufficient conditions. Historical conditions are neither necessary nor sufficient; there is nothing that compels this rather than that historical event to happen.

I have called this approach to historical method the 'Popper–Collingwood approach' because, despite the philosophical differences between them, the actual method prescribed by each seems to be substantially one and the same. I do not think it matters much for the pursuit of historical research whether one grafts on to historical explanations the vocabulary of hypothetico-deductivism, as long as one means nothing more specific than that the method involves a process of trial and error, something which few would deny.

If Popper means something more specific by his hypothetico-deductive account of rational reconstructions, he fails to make out any convincing argument for it. It is essential to the hypothetico-deductive method, as it is employed in natural science, that the research progresses by means of falsifications and corroborations from hypotheses of low generality to hypotheses of ever-increasing generality. In historical research the process is the reverse: it proceeds from general guesses to ever more specific hypotheses. The process involves trial and error, but it is not propelled by the kind of chance and unexpected falsifications or corroborations which form the most valuable evidence in natural science. An interpretative hypothesis in historical research is typically rejected not because it is false, but because it is formulated in concepts which are seen as inadequate to accommodate the available evidence. Resilient evidence does not so much call for the immediate rejection of a hypothesis as for a revision of the conceptual apparatus employed in the interpretation of the evidence. This interpretation of the evidence involves the proposal of new interpretative hypotheses which replace the older ones because of their higher interpretative adequacy. A head-on formal contradiction, not only between hypotheses and evidence, but even between rival hypotheses, is a luxury rarely met with in the human sciences.

Although my disagreement with Popper on this score may be of little consequence for the actual pursuit of historical research, it is, I believe, of the greatest consequence for general philosophical commitments. Popper's tenacity in linking the intellectual virtues of rationality and objectivity to the advocacy of the hypothetico-deductive method can only serve to bring those virtues in discredit among those who are concerned with the human sciences and are familiar with the methods of hermeneutic research. It has been one of my concerns in this essay to show that open-mindedness and respect for the weight of evidence are not inherently linked to the pursuit of the hypothetico-deductive method. This has been the reason for subjecting Popper's theory to detailed criticisms which might otherwise appear petty and trivial.

That the virtues of open-mindedness and respect for evidence are not the exclusive prerogative of hypothetico-deductivists seems amply borne out by Collingwood's analysis of the historical understanding. Documentary evidence, according to Collingwood, is not to be treated as a level of facts against which the historian tests his own detached hypotheses. Documents are primarily expressions of thoughts, with which the historian's own thoughts enter into discussion. The point of view of the historian is of interest for purposes of explanation only in so far as it is a point of view appropriate to the thoughts expressed in the documents. An 'appropriate' point of view does not necessarily mean the same point of view as that of the historical agent, but neither does it mean merely (as it does for Popper) a point of view consistent with the fact of the documentary evidence having been produced; what it means is a point of view from which it would be rational to think the thoughts expressed in the document with precisely the same 'force' or 'import' as that which they had for the agent. The *Theaetetus,* for instance, can be interpreted from the point of view of modern discussions of sensationalism, but it cannot be interpreted from the point of view of someone unfamiliar with, or indifferent to, epistemology.

In Popper's view, historical explanations are to be understood as higher-level hypotheses which are brought to bear on the documentary evidence 'from the outside', as it were. There can be a comparison of better or worse explanations of an event only given a particular preconceived point of view; there is no such thing as *the* explanation of an historical event. Popper's well-known formula 'there is no meaning in history' is meant, primarily, to summarize his polemic against teleological modes of thought; but Popper himself explicitly interprets it to mean that historical events have no significance in themselves; significance is imparted to them only through the preconceived selective point of view of the historian. Although Popper claims that history may conceivably retrogress, it is hard to see how, on his view, the history of thought can be rationally reconstructed as anything but a progression, culminating in the thought of the historian. This seems an inevitable consequence of using the historian's point of view as a yardstick for measuring the rationality of historical agents.

In Collingwood's view, it is the intensional content of the documents, and not the preferences or predilections of historians, that determines what constitutes an explanation of an historical event. While neither Collingwood nor Popper presupposes any sympathy or empathy with historical agents, Collingwood presupposes at least an intellectual involvement in their problems, something which Popper, at least in theory, considers superfluous. On Collingwood's view, too, history is to be reconstructed as a rational progression of human affairs; however, he believes that this is not a shortcoming imposed by the limited perspective of the historian's point of view, but that the progress is actually there in the historical process. This is a consequence of the principle of the continuity of the development of human thought. *Prima facie*, Popper may seem to be better off for repudiating the principle of continuity, but the price is a relativism which Popper himself abhors, but which – as I hope to have shown – he has never succeeded in freeing himself from. The relativism is inherent in his philosophy of science, in the thesis of conventionalism, and it can be eradicated only by the development of an alternative account of the factual basis of falsifications, for instance by the view that falsifications are based on our belief in the truth of basic statements. I have suggested that Popper would perhaps do well to adopt this line, since, in the last resort, he already has to fall back on his *belief* that falsifications bring us nearer to the truth in order to support his belief in the progress of science.

But if Popper is guilty of relativism, doesn't Collingwood succumb to the opposite pitfall? Isn't the principle of continuity an example of that kind of bad philosophical apriorism which one can adopt only arbitrarily and maintain only dogmatically? This question raises the more fundamental question of the relationship of philosophy to history. In a sense, if one wishes to employ the a priori–a posteriori dichotomy, the principle of continuity is a priori, since, on Collingwood's own view, history does not contain any level of pure, atheoretical facts which can be neatly separated from the theoretical activity of the historian and used as an independent testing-ground for the thoughts of the historian, or a fortiori those of the philosopher of history. But it does not follow that the principle of continuity is divorced from all experience, unless one adopts, a priori and arbitrarily, the dogma that all thought is either purely empirical and undiluted by theory, or else arbitrary. I see no reason to accept this dogma, and I see no insuperable objection to regarding the principle of continuity as a hermeneutic recommendation, to be validated by the extent to which it serves to render historical experience intelligible. Of course, it cannot meet with any straightforward falsification, since the principle prejudges the questions of whether, and by what canons of intelligibility, history ought to be rendered intelligible. These are not matters on which the philosopher can presume to dictate to the historian. Should he not then resign himself to relativism and placidly accept the verdicts of the historians? Well, what historians? There is no unanimous consensus to which to appeal. The majority of historians? But the real experts are always a minority. The best historians, then? Best by what standards?

Collingwood's answer is that the philosopher must himself be an historian in order to be able to do his job as a philosopher. The theoretical understanding of the historian's activity cannot be complete, and it cannot be formalized in a system. The theoretical understanding requires to be supplemented with the judicious insights to be gained only in the actual pursuit of historical research, insights which are neither infallible nor uncriticizable, but which are, nonetheless, as indispensable to the theoretician of history as they are to the working historian. This is why an essay of this format cannot finally answer the ultimate question of the truth and falsity of the conceptions of history here discussed, and this is why my discussion will not issue in the proposal of any comprehensive philosophical thesis of my own. The kind of logico-epistemological arguments that I have deployed can show in what respects the theories of Popper and Collingwood *cannot* be true, and in what respects they *may* be true. To seriously attempt to answer the question of whether Collingwood's theory actually *is* true, this study would need to be supplemented with a study of actual historical explanations, to be used not merely as examples, but to be seriously discussed in terms of their adequacy as historical explanations.

To show that I am not merely passing the buck, I try in the following Appendix to give an indication of the kind of discussion that would be required for this purpose. If I have been right in anything that I have said about the impossibility of a stratification of intellectual life, it follows that I cannot do this without to some extent committing myself on points of controversy among historians. I see no need to apologize for this; it should be sufficiently clear that I regard this trespass on the domain of historians as a prerequisite for judging the philosophical issues at stake.

Appendix: A Case Study

One of the most valuable maxims of Popper's ethics of research is, I believe, the maxim that a theory ought to be tested by its most remote consequences. It is easy to produce a rational reconstruction of the evolvement and defense of a scientific theory – even if it is a mistaken one, like Galileo's theory of the tides. The method of rational reconstruction, or situational analysis, is, one suspects, invented with precisely this kind of case in mind. A true test of its interpretative value would be whether we can produce a similar reconstruction of a phenomenon which, *prima facie,* seems utterly beyond the bounds of reason. Here, I want to focus on Stalin's mass terror, a seemingly quite irrational phenomenon, which has evoked an intriguing variety of responses from historians.

A number of brilliant examples of situational analyses are to be found in George F. Kennan's *Russia and the West under Lenin and Stalin.*[1] Kennan's chief concern is the deterioration of East–West diplomacy following the October Revolution. One question which he faces is: Why was the Soviet Union from the beginning hostile, suspicious, and uncooperative toward the progressive, liberal, and democratic regime of the US? Here is a seemingly irrational phenomenon, 'hostility to the forces of goodness and decency', which seems to require a causal, socio-psychological explanation. Instead Kennan endeavors to show that the very description of the Russian reaction is ill-conceived. The Russian hostility was not directed against the US as the embodiment of liberalism and democracy; it was directed against the US as one of the Allied powers which put pressure on Russia to stay in a war which Russia had neither the interest nor the ability to continue. The Russians did not 'misunderstand the good intentions' of the US; they understood perfectly well that the US had

99

intentions that were ruinous to Russia; specifically, the intention to maintain the Eastern front until the Germans surrendered.

Russian hostility to the West has been commonly explained by the Russians themselves as mere self-defense against repeated attacks on the Soviet Union by the world bourgeoisie. Most frequently cited in this connection are the Allied interventions in the Russian Civil War. These interventions are typically conceived of as concerted all-out efforts on the part of the world bourgeoisie to overthrow the Soviet government and destroy socialism. In short, the interventions are characterized as a basically irrational phenomenon, to be causally explained by the limited class interests of the bourgeoisie. Against this, Kennan opposes an alternative characterization of the phenomenon to be explained. In the first place, the Russian characterization of the interventions ignores the highly interesting fact that there was a world war going on at the time; in the second place, there was no concerted all-out effort, only limited-purpose efforts, reluctantly and hesitantly undertaken. The most important were the British North Russian intervention and the US Siberian intervention. The North Russian intervention was undertaken at the request of the Murmansk Soviet, in order to defend Murmansk against the advancing Germans. The British could hardly foresee that the Murmansk Soviet would shortly fall out with Moscow, and that the British troops, therefore, would have to fight Russian Bolsheviks. Similarly, the US intervention in Siberia was undertaken in order to evacuate the Czechoslovak Corps, which was reported to have been cut off by a volunteer army of German POW's. Wilson, who made the decision to intervene, was plainly unaware that the Czechs had no desire to be evacuated and that the actual opponents were not Germans but Russian Bolsheviks. In both cases, the intervention troops were embroiled in (light and insignificant) combat with Red Guards, but in neither case was this expected or understood by the governments that sent the troops in. Hence, for purposes of interpretation, the formula 'effort at overthrowing the Soviet government' is an erroneous characterization of the action which the Allied governments were engaged in. This is not to say that the Allied governments might not have wanted to overthrow the Soviet government; the French certainly did want just that; the point is that the Allied interventions can be fully explained and understood without any reference to such a motive.

So far, Kennan's explanations are prototypes of rational reconstructions. In both the cases described he encounters seemingly irrational phenomena and shows that the action concerned must be characterized in different terms, as a consequence of which the reasonableness of the action becomes apparent, and the need for a causal explanation is seen to disappear. When he comes to dealing with the Stalin period, however, Kennan is unable to maintain this approach. Stalin's foreign and domestic policies are explained as due to a morbid suspiciousness, stemming from the inferiority complex of a provincial Georgian toward Western diplomats, as well as toward the suave, Western-bred Bolshevik leaders. This not uncommon explanation is characteristically a *causal* explanation. The trouble with such an explanation, from the theoretical point of view expounded in this essay, is that it does not render the Stalinist phenomenon intelligible; rather, the appeal to psychological causes contains an admission that this phenomenon belongs to the realm of irrational actions, which we cannot presume to fully understand. For all that, it may well be a true explanation; the philosopher can have no a priori grounds on which to dismiss it. However, the hermeneutic principle that historical actions ought to be reconstructed as the rational response to problem-situations impels us to look for a rational reconstruction of Stalin's actions that would render Stalin's personal mental history superfluous for purposes of historical explanation. Needless to say, the failure to come up with such a reconstruction will have to be put on record as a *prima facie* limitation on our hermeneutic principle.

The most impressive attempt, to date, at giving a rational reconstruction of Stalinism is, by common consent, Isaac Deutscher's great biography of Stalin.[2] The book has won acclaim for its supreme detachment; though basically hostile toward Stalin, Deutscher sets out neither to condemn nor to praise, but simply to understand. Deutscher's fundamental thesis is that the terror and repression of the thirties was the price paid for rapid industrialization in a backward agrarian country. On Soviet Russia's 'second revolution', Deutscher writes: 'It resulted in Russia's rapid industrialization; it compelled more than a hundred million peasants to abandon their small, primitive holdings and to set up collective farms; it ruthlessly tore the primeval wooden plough from the hands of the muzhik and forced him to grasp the wheel of a modern tractor; it drove tens of millions of illiterate people to school and made them learn to read and write; and spiritually it detached European Russia from Europe and brought Asiatic Russia nearer to Europe. The rewards of that revolution were astounding; but so was its cost: the complete loss, by a whole generation, of spiritual and political freedom.'[3] Of course, if we can make sense of the claim that industrialization was achieved at the cost of political freedom, then Stalin's choice to initiate repression might be viewed as a rational one — however morally repulsive – and there would be no need to inquire further into Stalin's personal psyche.

How does Deutscher make out the case for this connection? He deals with the terror chiefly under two headings: the crash collectivization of 1929–30, and the Purge Trials of 1936–38. The collectivization is explained as follows. By 1928, the Soviet government had achieved a fairly successful industrial growth, but it had not been matched by a similar growth in agricultural output. By 1928, the cities were threatened by imminent famine; the peasants were reluctant to supply food for the cities; continued industrialization demanded that the industrial workers be fed; hence, force had to be applied. This explanation is of course somewhat weakened by the obvious observation that collectivization in fact brought about a foreseeable, deliberately created famine of unspeakable proportions. Deutscher attempts to get around this by claiming that Stalin vacillated too long before making up his mind on the collectivization issue. In the process of seizing power he had to defend two alternative views in succession, in order to play the Right and the Left against each other. By the time he was in power the food situation had been aggravated to the point where he was in a dilemma: there was no way of avoiding famine, no matter what he did. 'If the Government had begun to curb the big farmers and to encourage gradual collectivization earlier, as Trotsky and Zinoviev had counselled, it might not have needed now to resort to drastic emergency measures in order to obtain bread. As things stood, Stalin acted under the overwhelming pressure of events. The circumstance that he was not prepared for the events precipitated him into a course of action over which he was liable to lose control.'[4] Evidently, the claim that the repressive measures of collectivization – 5 to 6 million casualties – was the price of industrialization and agricultural reform, has here been rather seriously qualified. Events got beyond Stalin's control because, at the time when he might have been able to influence them, he had been too busy using the agricultural issue to play Bukharin against Zinoviev. What Deutscher is really saying, without seeming quite to realize it, is that Stalin sacrificed 5 to 6 million lives simply in order to satisfy his own desire for absolute power. This implication throws us back on a psychological explanation of Stalin's character.

Stalin's second *tour de force*, the Purge Trials, is discussed in greater detail. The rationale, Deutscher admits, was the consolidation of Stalin's personal power, but that does not necessarily mean power for its own sake: 'It is not necessary to assume that he acted from sheer cruelty or lust for power. He may be given the dubious credit of the sincere conviction that what he did served the interests of the revolution and that he alone interpreted those interests aright.'[5] There were, according to Deutscher, two perfectly rational purposes for which Stalin may have considered his personal dictatorship necessary, industrialization and the defense against Germany.

During the early thirties Russia, under Stalin's leadership, underwent a rapid and impressive industrial expansion. Measured in human lives and suffering, the Russian industrial revolution may well have been wasteful and inefficient, but it was rapid, and it did achieve results. Now Deutscher's argument is that Stalin was able to carry out this crash industrialization only by gathering all power into his own hands and stifling all opposition. His Bolshevik comrades resented his autocratic methods of government, and they represented a real threat to his authority; hence they had to be disposed of by some sort of repressive means. '[Stalin] "built socialism"; and even his opponents, while denouncing his autocracy, admitted that most of his economic reforms were indeed essential for socialism. The revenge of the past thus bore not so much on his social programme as on his technique of government.'[6] In this, Deutscher suggests, Stalin may be compared to Dostoyevsky's Grand Inquisitor, who renounced Christ's teachings and 'corrected his work', in order to achieve practical results.

The chief trouble with this line of argument is that the peak of terror and repression was reached in the years 1937–38, while the crash industrialization programme was on the whole completed by 1935. Indeed, the Purges actually hindered further industrial growth, since the victims numbered, among others, precisely those talented entrepreneurs and engineers who made industrialization a success, and who were now replaced by subservient, unenterprising mediocrities. This is made amply clear by Robert Conquest, in *The Great Terror:* 'the basic economic benefits obtained, or supposedly obtained, by the Stalin regime were already in hand before the Purge proper started. Economically, in fact, there is no doubt that the Purge was disadvantageous: it removed a high proportion of the most skilled industrial leaders, from Pyatakov down; and at the same time the camps were filled from an already overstretched labour pool.'[7] Conquest may be suspected of an anti-Communist bias; but no such suspicion attaches to the Marxist-Leninist historian Roy Medvedev, who arrives at exactly the same conclusion, in his work *Let History Judge:* 'By his crimes Stalin did not help, he hindered, he did not accelerate, he slowed down the people's movement to socialism and communism in the Soviet Union and in the whole world. In some respects Stalin even turned this movement backward.'[8]

On Deutscher's argument, however, Stalin needed dictatorial power in order to industrialize and to 'build socialism'; the main threat towards his power was connected with the rise of Nazism in Germany. From 1936 on, it seemed inevitable that Soviet Russia must either reach an entente with Nazi Germany or risk a military showdown; either eventuality would provide Stalin's opponents with a welcome opportunity of deposing him. In the Purge Trials, Stalin falsely accused his rivals of having entered into secret treaties with Hitler; here, Deutscher surmises, Stalin accused his enemies of already having done what he suspected they would do, if given the opportunity: 'His reasoning probably developed along the following lines: they may want to overthrow me in a crisis – I shall charge them with already having made the attempt. They certainly believe themselves to be better fitted for the conduct of war, which is absurd. A change of government may weaken Russia's fighting capacity; and if they succeed, they may be compelled to sign a truce with Hitler, and perhaps even agree to a cession of territory as we once did at Brest Litovsk. I shall accuse them of having already entered into a treacherous alliance with Germany (and Japan) and ceded Soviet territory to those states.'[9]

If Stalin's reasoning probably developed along such lines, we should have a kind of rational interpretation of the Purge Trials. But how probable is it? How likely is it that Stalin in 1936 worried that 'a change of government might weaken Russia's fighting capacity', considering that he did not worry, in 1937, about whether the elimination of one fourth of the officers' corps might not weaken the fighting capacity? How seriously could Stalin have taken the threat of war in 1936, when he was caught entirely unprepared in 1941? And why should Stalin have been unduly worried about a second Brest Litovsk, when he himself, in 1939, was quite ready to sign the Nazi–Soviet Nonaggression pact?

Furthermore, this kind of explanation presupposes that Stalin's terror was a more or less isolated episode, concentrated in the years 1936–38. Those were indeed the peak years. But it was in the late forties that Sartre's conscience began bothering him about the labor camps; it was in 1945–46 that these camps were filled with returning Russian POW's; it was in 1948 that the scientific community was purged of geneticists; and it was in 1953 that Stalin planned the pogrom of the Jews. On the other hand, the first 'wreckers' trial, the Promparty Trial, took place in 1930, at a time when Stalin, through the Comintern, was busy eliminating all obstacles to Hitler's rise to power.

There is a more fundamental objection to Deutscher's entire line of argument. Neither industrialization nor war preparation would make sense of the Purges unless there existed, in 1936, a real or perceived threat to Stalin's hegemony. By a 'perceived threat' I mean one which would be perceived as such by most reasonable men. Paranoiacs, of course, perceive threats everywhere. Now Deutscher claims that Stalin had good reasons to feel threatened; in the ranks of younger Party members, there was a rebellious spirit, which expressed itself in occasional acts of terrorism, such as the assassination of Sergei Kirov in Leningrad in 1934. Kirov's assassin entered his office unobstructed; Kirov's security staff were obviously guilty of foul play; if this could happen to Stalin's deputy in Leningrad, it might happen to Stalin. 'The assassination of Kirov alarmed Stalin. Had not conspirators penetrated into his own office?'[10] 'Stalin drew the conclusion that the time for quasi-liberal concessions was over. His victory over the opposition had been far from complete. He had only succeeded in driving discontent from the surface to the depths of political life. He would now strike deeper and harder.'[11]

Unfortunately, all the evidence now available indicates that Stalin personally ordered the murder of Kirov. This was explicitly asserted by the former chekist Alexander Orlov in 1954,[12] and, as Conquest points out,[13] the same conclusion was clearly implied by Khrushchev, in his 1956 and 1961 speeches. It can no longer be supposed that Stalin was 'alarmed' by the Kirov murder. This realization undercuts Deutscher's attempt at portraying the Purge as essentially an act of self-defense. To sum up my discussion of Deutscher: his reconstruction of Stalinism, though eminently reasonable and persuasive, constantly goes against the facts. We clearly do not want a rational reconstruction if it has to be bought at the price of major inaccuracies and neglect of pertinent facts. The question which we are now forced to face is: Given all the objections to Deutscher's reconstruction, do we really want a rational reconstruction of Stalinism at all? Do we really want to understand Stalinism; is it not the kind of phenomenon where we expect, and readily accept, a certain lack of intelligibility? If it is, does this not show the inapplicability – or at least the poverty – of the 'Popper–Collingwood approach' to historical explanation?

These negative conclusions seem to be supported by a comparison of Deutscher's work with that of Conquest. Conquest's approach is not that of the philosopher, but that of the journalist. With an amazing array of detailed facts, he systematically demolishes the various rational explanations that have been offered from time to time, on the grounds of economics, national defense, etc. We have seen how Deutscher's explanation fares when subjected to this kind of criticism. As presented by Conquest, the Purges and the labor camps make sense from one point of view only, the point of view of Stalin's despotic designs. But this is equivalent to saying that they make no sense: The desire to possess absolute power, for its own sake, is not commonly recognized as a rational desire, and whatever has to be explained in terms of such a desire is not explained in rational terms, but in terms of psychological causation. Fundamentally, Conquest's story is the story of a succession of disastrous contingencies, 'a tale full of sound and fury, signifying nothing'.

I do not find it possible to controvert Conquest on questions of fact, and I do not think it possible to 'save' the hermeneutic principle of rational reconstruction by trying to read some deeper rationality into Stalin's actions. On the other hand, I am not sure that the principle requires such a stratagem. The argument may be made that, by attributing Stalin's actions to an irrational mind, one has not 'explained' Stalin's actions historically; what one has done is remove

106

Stalin's actions from the sphere of the historically significant, and thereby shifted the historically interesting question from 'Why did Stalin act as he did?' to 'Why did the Soviet Union tolerate the emergence and perpetuation of Stalin's leadership?'. And it is not clear that the second question cannot be answered by the method of rational reconstruction.

How this problem-shift forces itself on the working historian is particularly clear from R. Medvedev's work *Let History Judge.* Like the majority of the present-day 'left wing' Russian intelligentsia, Medvedev abhors Stalinism, while he regards the Lenin age as a Golden Age of humanitarianism, democracy, and legality. From this point of view, Medvedev finds it necessary to place the responsibility for Stalinism solely on Stalin himself, but this, of course, entails that the transformation of Soviet government from Leninism to Stalinism becomes a phenomenon requiring a special explanation. Being a Leninist and an anti-Stalinist, Medvedev naturally finds it impossible to explain the emergence of Stalinism as being in any sense rational; instead, he resorts to a causal, sociological explanation, listing a number of social conditions which facilitated Stalin's rise to power, such as the cult of personality, the secrecy of governmental procedures, the general backwardness of Russia's political culture, etc. These conditions, Medvedev stresses, are not sufficient; Stalin's rise to power is causally undetermined, and must, in the last resort, be put down as a tragic historical accident.

The shortcomings of this approach are elucidated by an examination of a work by Roy Medvedev's twin brother, Zhores Medvedev, on a particular aspect of Stalinism, the perversion of biology under the reign of Lysenko. In *The Rise and Fall of T. D. Lysenko,*[14] Medvedev repeatedly stresses that Lysenkoism, unlike any other scientific theory, gained ascendancy not through open discussion, but through the repression of scientific discussion. When discussion of genetics was again permitted, from 1964 on, Lysenkoism rapidly lost its following within the scientific community. Medvedev's explanation of the rise of Lysenkoism is this: In the normal course of research, false theories appear all the time, but they are normally weeded out through discussion and criticism. In this case, the authoritarian structure of the state and Stalin's all-pervasive regimentation brought discussion to a halt, which facilitated the perpetuation of a disastrously false theory, which held a monopoly for more than two decades.

So far, so good. But the reader cannot help feeling that there is something missing from Medvedev's account. Lysenko's main argument in support of his theory was that it was based on dialectical materialism. Medvedev cites this claim but, although he discusses the application of Lysenkoism to all fields of agriculture, he never once takes up the question of the theory's relationship to dialectical materialism. The reason for this omission is both simple and obvious. As Jacques Monod has pointed out,[15] on the presuppositions of dialectical materialism, Lysenko was right and the geneticists wrong. Lysenko's claim that acquired traits are inheritable satisfies Engels's theory that nature evolves through the interaction of the organism with its environment; on the other hand, the Mendelist theory of the invariant transmission of genes through thousands of generations is nonsense from the point of view of dialectics. In other words, in an open and honest discussion between dialectical materialists, Lysenkoism *ought to* have defeated Mendelism. The fact that the Mendelists were not convinced but only silenced through repression, suggests either that they were insincere dialectical materialists, or that their biological and philosophical beliefs were inconsistent. At any rate, once the consistency of Lysenkoism with dialectical materialism is recognized, we no longer need a special explanation of Lysenkoism, although we may want an explanation of the rise of dialectical materialism.

This rational reconstruction of the rise of Lysenkoism may be tentatively extended to the explanation of the rise of Stalinism. The question is: Is the rise to absolute power on the part of one ruthless, unprincipled man rationally explicable on any of the presuppositions of Leninism? Not surprisingly, this is precisely the question taken up by Conquest, who has followed up his momumental work on Stalin's terror with a shorter study of Lenin. It is, of course, widely recognized that Lenin's most significant intellectual and political legacy is the incorporation in Marxism of the vanguard conception of a single, tightly disciplined Party. It is likewise widely acknowledged that the success of the October Revolution was largely due to the Party organization instituted by Lenin. Now Conquest's argument is that Lenin's centralized Party was capable of coping only with the problems of revolution, and not with those of 'normal' government. Bred in a country which lacked a civic tradition, Lenin had developed a philosophy which aimed only at overthrowing tyranny, not at solving the everyday problems of democracy: 'In Lenin's pre-revolutionary works there is no sign of any awareness of the fact that in *any* political régime there are certain precautions to be taken, certain rules to be observed – and certain lessons to be learnt from the politics of the past. In his post-revolutionary writings, the problems of real politics, and the corruption of power and the establishment of interests, come to him as a constant shock to which he can only suggest piecemeal and (as it turned out) useless remedies. ... In fact Lenin had no *political* philosophy covering a post-revolutionary period, no notion that a proletarian democracy might require any system of sanctions to control its representatives. The gap was filled by authoritarian expediency.'[16]

The claim is not that Stalinist conclusions are strictly and inevitably deducible from Leninist premises, but that there was a lacuna in Lenin's philosophy which had to be filled with *something* after the Revolution. The recipe for socialist government was incomplete and Lenin's successors had to improvise; however, it was sufficiently definite to place narrow limits on the scope of the improvisation. It was precisely their strict adherence to Leninism that, at the critical moment, deterred Bukharin and Rykov from preventing Stalin's assumption of power. The critical juncture, Conquest holds, was in 1930, following the abysmal failure of collectivization: 'Under any other system, it would have been the time for the Rightist leaders to stand forward. Their warnings had proved correct. But they made no effort to achieve power. Bukharin and Rykov and the others explicitly condemned any question of standing against "the Party" – that is, against the Congresses and Central Committees which Stalin's Secretariat had packed. As for the question of a united front with other socialist forces, they rejected such an idea with horror, precisely on Leninist principles.'[17] The point here is not, of course, that Bukharin and Rykov were psychologically conditioned by their adherence to Leninism, but that, on their Leninist presuppositions, their course of action– or inaction – seemed a reasonable one; likewise, to an historian with knowledge of those presuppositions, their attitude is intelligible and, in that sense, 'predictable'.

That Conquest is not advancing a causal hypothesis, in any deterministic sense, is made amply clear: 'Only believers in historical inevitability would argue that Stalin was inevitable, that he was simply and solely Lenin's heir. But it is at least clear that no very liberal character could have come to lead the Party; that, as a result of the way in which Lenin left the Party organised, it was likely to fall into the hand of the best manipulator of the apparatus.'[18] So the principles of Leninism entail, not Stalinism, but the establishment of institutional conditions which were likely to produce a leader with scant respect for legality or for the opinions of others. In those principles, therefore, we find a point of view from which it *might* be rational to yield power to a criminally insane man; thus we may be said to have also achieved historical understanding of those actions which were to flow from Stalin's deranged mind. In so far as one accepts this interpretation, one will have vindicated the principle of rational reconstruction in the face of a highly recalcitrant example.

This interpretation is, admittedly, controversial. In a sense this is as it should be. A hermeneutic principle should not depend solely on non-controversial cases; to be of any interest to historians it must have something to say about controversial issues in historiography. In this appendix I hope to have shown two things of general interest. In the first place, philosophers cannot resolve meta-questions of historical method without taking a stand in actual historical disputes; hence, their questions are not merely meta-questions. In the second place, historians cannot remain indifferent to theoretical disputes concerning the nature of historical explanations; hence, their questions are not merely factual. In this sense, the young Collingwood seems to have been right when summing up the relationship of philosophy to history: 'Each alike must also be the other or it cannot be itself; each in being itself is also the other.'[19]

Notes

INTRODUCTION

1 Carl G. Hempel, 'Explanations in Science and in History', in W. H. Dray, ed., *Philosophical Analysis and History* (Harper & Row, New York, 1966), p. 103.
2 William H. Dray, *Laws and Explanation in History* (Oxford, 1957), pp. 164 ff.

2. POPPER'S PROGRAM IN THE LOGIC OF SCIENCE

1 Imre Lakatos, 'Popper on demarcation and induction', in P. A. Schilpp, ed., *The Philosophy of Karl R. Popper* (Open Court, Glencoe, Ill., 1973).
2 Karl R. Popper, *The Logic of Scientific Discovery* (Harper & Row, New York, 1959), p. 41.
3 Ibid., p. 86.
4 A. J. Ayer, *Language, Truth and Logic* (Dover, New York, 1952), p. 95
5 Otto von Neurath, 'Pseudorationalismus der Falsifikation', *Erkenntnis 5*, 1935.
6 Popper, op.cit., p. 43.
7 Ibid., pp. 95—105.
8 Ibid., p. 108.
9 Ibid., p. 111.
10 Ibid., p. 277.
11 Popper, *Conjectures and Refutations* (Basic Books, New York, 1962), p. 199.

3. THE FRUITFULNESS OF HISTORICISM

1 Popper, *The Poverty of Historicism* (Harper & Row, New York, 1964), p. 3.
2 Popper, *The Open Society and its Enemies*, vol. 2 (Harper & Row, New York, 1963), p. 208.
3 Maurice Mandelbaum, *The Problem of Historical Knowledge* (Harper & Row, New York, 1967), pp. 88—89. Before this, the term 'historicism' was used in the same sense by Lord Acton, in his 1895 Inaugural Lecture. Cf. his *Lectures on Modern History* (Fontana, London, 1960), p. 36.
4 Ibid., p. 89.
5 Popper, *Conjectures and Refutations*, op.cit., p. 129.
6 *The Open Society*, vol. 2, pp. 216—17.
7 Ibid., p. 217.
8 Thomas S. Kuhn, *The Structure of Scientific Revolutions* (Univ. of Chicago Press, Chicago, Ill., 1962).
9 *The Open Society*, vol. 2, p. 218.
10 *The Poverty of Historicism*, p. 145.

11 Alan Donagan, 'Explanation in History', in P. Gardiner, ed., *Theories of History* (The Free Press, New York, 1959).
12 *The Open Society*, vol. 2. pp. 363—64.
13 *The Poverty of Historicism*, p. 149.
14 Ibid.
15 Ibid., p. 150.
16 *The Open Society*, vol. 1, p. 170.
17 Ibid., p. 171.

4. FROM HISTORY TO METAPHYSICS

1 Popper, *The Open Society*, vol. 2, p. 369.
2 Popper, *Objective Knowledge; An Evolutionary Approach* (Oxford, 1972), p. 328. Cf. in this connection Alfred Tarski, 'The semantic conception of truth and the foundations of semantics'. in Feigl & Sellars, eds., *Readings in Philosophical Analysis* (Appleton-Century-Crofts, New York, 1949).
3 *The Open Society*, vol. 2. p. 373.
4 Ibid.
5 *Objective Knowledge*, p. 335.
6 *The Open Society*, vol. 2, pp. 375—76.
7 Ibid., p. 377.
8 *Objective Knowledge*, p. 106.
9 Ibid., p. 107.
10 Ibid., p. 170.
11 Ibid., p. 171.
12 Ibid., p. 174.
13 Ibid., pp. 176—77.
14 Ibid., p. 177.
15 Ibid., p. 107.

5. POPPER'S DISPUTE WITH COLLINGWOOD

1 Popper, *Objective Knowledge*, pp. 187—88.
2 Joseph Agassi. 'Towards an Historiography of Science', *History and Theory*, 2, 1963, p. 50.
3 *Objective Knowledge*, pp. 163—64.
4 R. G. Collingwood, *Religion and Philosophy* (Macmillan, London, 1916), p. 42.
5 Collingwood, *An Essay on Metaphysics* (Oxford, 1940), p. 119.
6 *Objective Knowledge*, p. 187.
7 Ibid., p. 188.
8 Ibid., p. 177.
9 Ibid., p. 178.
10 Ibid.

6. INVENTORY OF THE THIRD WORLD

1 Anthony Quinton, 'Sir Karl Popper; Knowledge as an Institution', *Encounter*, December 1973, pp. 35—36.
2 Gottlob Frege, 'On Sense and Reference', in P. T. Geach & M. Black, eds., *Translations From the Philosophical Writings of Gottlob Frege* (Blackwell, Oxford, 1966). p. 57.
3 Ibid., p. 62.
4 Ibid., p. 59.

5 Ibid., p. 69.
6 Ibid.
7 Bertrand Russell, 'On Denoting', in Marsh, ed., *Logic and Knowledge* (Capricorn, New York, 1971), pp. 48—49.
8 Ibid., p. 50.
9 Frege, 'The Thought: A Logical Inquiry', in P. F. Strawson, ed., *Philosophical Logic* (Oxford, 1967), p. 29.
10 Ibid., p. 20.
11 Ibid., p. 23.
12 Ibid., p. 24.
13 Ibid., p. 25.
14 Ibid.
15 Ibid., p. 24.

7. COLLINGWOOD'S PHILOSOPHY OF MIND

1 Louis O. Mink, *Mind, History and Dialectic: The Philosophy of R. G. Collingwood* (Indiana Univ. Press, Bloomington, Ind.. 1969).
2 Lionel Rubinoff, *Collingwood and the Reform of Metaphysics: A Study in the Philosophy of Mind* (Univ. of Toronto Press, Toronto, 1970).
3 Collingwood, *Religion and Philosophy*. p. 34.
4 Ibid., p. 100.
5 Ibid., p. 101.
6 Ibid.
7 Ibid., p. 46.
8 Ibid., p. 42.
9 Collingwood, *Speculum Mentis* (Oxford, 1924), p. 255.

8. THE THEORY OF PRESUPPOSITIONS I: AN INTERPRETATION

1 Collingwood, *An Autobiography,* p. 25.
2 Ibid., p. 33.
3 Ibid., p. 38.
4 Ibid., p. 31.
5 Collingwood, *An Essay on Metaphysics*, p. 23.
6 Ibid., p. 24.
7 P. F. Strawson, 'On Referring', in C. E. Caton, ed., *Philosophy and Ordinary Language* (Univ. of Illinois Press, Chicago, Ill., 1963). P. Grice, 'Meaning', in Strawson, *Philosophical Logic*.
8 J. L. Austin, *How To Do Things With Words* (Oxford, 1965). John R. Searle, *Speech Acts* (Cambridge, 1969).
9 Noam Chomsky, *Aspects of the Theory of Syntax* (MIT Press, Cambridge, Mass., 1965).
10 I owe this example to a lecture by Professor Alasdair MacIntyre.
11 *An Essay on Metaphysics*, p. 26.

9. THE THEORY OF PRESUPPOSITIONS II: CRITICAL RESERVATIONS

1 Max Weber, *The Theory of Social and Economic Organization* (The Free Press, New York, 1964), p. 92.

2 W. H. Walsh, *Metaphysics* (Harcourt, Brace & World Inc., New York, 1963), p. 172.
  Stephen Toulmin, 'Conceptual Revolutions in Science', in *Boston Studies in The Philosophy of Science,* 1964—66, vol. III (Dordrecht, 1967).
3 Collingwood, *An Essay on Philosophical Method* (Oxford, 1933), p. 195.
4 Collingwood, *An Autobiography,* p. 62.
5 Collingwood, *An Essay on Metaphysics,* pp. 29, 31.
6 Ibid., p. 48.
7 Peter Skagestad, 'Collingwood's Theory of Presuppositions: Its Origins and Development and Contemporary Philosophical Significance'; Ph.D. dissertation, Brandeis University, Waltham, Mass., 1973, especially Chapter 4.

10. THE RE-ENACTMENT OF THE PAST

1 Collingwood, *The Idea of History* (Oxford, 1946), p. 286.
2 Ibid., p. 292.
3 Ibid., p. 218.
4 Ibid., p. 289.
5 Ibid., p. 301.
6 Gilbert Ryle, *The Concept of Mind* (London, 1949), pp. 33, 46.
7 P. T. Geach, *Mental Acts* (Routledge & Kegan Paul, London. 1957), pp. 80 ff.

APPENDIX: A CASE STUDY

1 George F. Kennan, *Russia and the West under Lenin and Stalin* (New American Library, New York, 1961).
2 Isaac Deutscher, *Stalin* (Penguin, Harmondsworth 1966).
3 Ibid., p. 296.
4 Ibid.. p. 319.
5 Ibid., pp. 374—75.
6 Ibid., p. 358.
7 Robert Conquest, *The Great Terror* (Penguin, Harmondsworth, 1971), p. 661.
8 Roy A. Medvedev, *Let History Judge* (Random House, New York, 1971), p. xxxi.
9 Deutscher, op.cit., p. 374.
10 Ibid., p. 355.
11 Ibid., p. 353.
12 Alexander Orlov, *The Secret History of Stalin's Crimes* (London, 1954).
13 Conquest, op.cit., pp. 80—81.
14 Zhores A. Medvedev, *The Rise and Fall of T. D. Lysenko* (Doubleday, New York, 1971), especially pp. 248—54.
15 Jacques Monod, *Tilfeldigheten og Nødvendigheten* (Gyldendal, Oslo, 1972), p. 42.
16 Conquest, *Lenin* (Fontana, London, 1972), pp. 120—22.
17 Ibid., p. 125.
18 Ibid., p. 126.
19 Collingwood, *Religion and Philosophy,* p. 52.

Bibliography

Joseph Agassi, 'Towards an Historiography of Science', *History and Theory 2*, 1963.

J. L. Austin, *How To Do Things With Words*, Oxford, 1965.

A. J. Ayer, *Language, Truth and Logic*, Dover, New York, 1952.

Boston Studies in the Philosophy of Science 1964—66, vol. III Dordrecht, 1967.

Charles E. Caton, *Philosophy and Ordinary Language*, Univ. of Chicago Press, Chicago, Ill., 1963.

Noam Chomsky, *Aspects of the Theory of Syntax*, MIT Press, Cambridge, Mass., 1965.

R. G. Collingwood,
An Autobiography, Oxford, 1939.
An Essay on Metaphysics, Oxford, 1940.
An Essay on Philosophical Method, Oxford, 1933.
Religion and Philosophy, Macmillan, London, 1916.
Speculum Mentis, Oxford, 1924.
The Idea of History, Oxford, 1946.
The Idea of Nature, Oxford, 1945.

Robert Conquest,
Lenin, Fontana, London, 1972.
The Great Terror, Penguin, Harmondsworth, 1971.

Isaac Deutscher, *Stalin*, Penguin, Harmondsworth, 1966.

William H. Dray, *Laws and Explanation in History*, Oxford, 1957.
Philosophical Analysis and History, Harper & Row, New York, 1966.

Patrick Gardiner, *Theories of History*, The Free Press, New York, 1959.

P. T. Geach, *Mental Acts*, Routledge & Kegan Paul, London, 1957.
And Max Black, eds., *Translations from the Philosophical Writings of Gottlob Frege*, Blackwell, Oxford, 1966.

George F. Kennan, *Russia and the West under Lenin and Stalin*, New American Library, New York, 1961.

Thomas S. Kuhn, *The Structure of Scientific Revolutions*, Univ. of Chicago Press, Chicago, Ill., 1962.

Maurice Mandelbaum, *The Problem of Historical Knowledge*, Harper & Row, New York, 1967.

Roy A. Medvedev, *Let History Judge*, Random House, New York, 1971.

Zhores A. Medvedev, *The Rise and Fall of T. D. Lysenko*, Doubleday, New York, 1971.

Louis O. Mink, *Mind, History and Dialectic: The Philosophy of R. G. Collingwood*, Indiana Univ. Press, Bloomington, Ind., 1969.

Jacques Monod, *Tilfeldigheten og Nødvendigheten*, Gyldendal, Oslo, 1972.

115

Alexander Orlov, *The Secret History of Stalin's Crimes*, London, 1954.

Karl R. Popper,
Conjectures and Refutations, Basic Books, New York, 1962.
Objective Knowledge: An Evolutionary Approach, Oxford, 1972.
The Logic of Scientific Discovery, Harper & Row, New York, 1959.
The Open Society and its Enemies, Harper & Row, New York, 1963.
The Poverty of Historicism, Harper & Row, New York, 1964.

Lionel Rubinoff, *Collingwood and the Reform of Metaphysics: An Essay in the Philosophy of Mind*, Univ. of Toronto Press, Toronto, 1970.

Bertrand Russell, *Logic and Knowledge*, Capricorn, New York, 1971.

Gilbert Ryle, *The Concept of Mind*, London, 1949.

P. A. Schilpp, ed., *The Philosophy of Karl R. Popper*, Open Court, Glencoe, Ill., 1973.

John Searle, *Speech Acts*, Cambridge, 1969.

Peter Skagestad, R. G. Collingwood's Theory of Presuppositions, Ph.D. dissertation, Brandeis Univ., Waltham, Mass., 1973.

P. F. Strawson, *Philosophical Logic*, Oxford, 1967.

W. H. Walsh, *Metaphysics*, Harcourt, Brace & World Inc., New York, 1963.

Max Weber, *The Theory of Social and Economic Organization*, The Free Press, New York, 1964.

Index